W9-BGK-670

6. 50
9 12

Songs to Birds

Songs to Birds

ESSAYS BY
JAKE PAGE

Illustrations by Wesley W. Bates

DAVID R. GODINE
Publisher · Boston

First published in 1993 by
DAVID R. GODINE, PUBLISHER, INC.
Horticultural Hall
300 Massachusetts Avenue
Boston, Massachusetts 02115

Copyright © 1993 Jake Page

All rights reserved. No part of this book may be
used or reproduced in any manner whatsoever without written
permission, except in the case of brief quotations
embodied in critical articles and reviews.

Library of Congress Cataloging-in-Publication Data
Page, Jake.
Songs to birds: essays / Jake Page. – 1st ed.
p.   cm.
ISBN 0-87923-957-3
1. Birds – Behavior. 2. Animal communication. I. Title.
QL698.3.P32   1993   92-39278
598 – dc20   CIP

FIRST EDITION
Manufactured in the United States of America

For my birds

∾ ↭

Dana, Lindsey,
Sally, Lea,
Kendall, and Brooke

Contents

Introduction

SOMEONE, PROBABLY SOCRATES, once said that the unexamined life is not worth living. Today a lot of people spend vast parts of their time examining their lives in such minute detail that self-examination bids fair to become the modern equivalent of gluttony. Indeed, it is a major industry. Socrates, or whoever, was clever: in one statement, he threw a huge guilt trip on those of us who more or less languorously try to let the present be the present and, from time to time, simply lie back and enjoy the pageant without any particular attempt to derive lessons from it. Also, he simultaneously dismissed most lives on earth – such as those of birds – as not worth living, for it is unlikely that any bird is capable of a great deal of self-examination. But in my aimless way I think bird lives *are* worth living – for themselves, for the planet, and even for me. Imagine a beach without shore birds. There would be life in the water and in the sand, but nothing really to see as you loll on your beach towel. No cat-and-mouse game played with the surf's edge by sandpipers; no swooping of gulls. Just the inanity of pure geophysics: pointless waves. Give me some unexamined lives, full of purpose, and the time simply to lie back and enjoy them.

Of course, there are lessons to be learned from birds as from nearly everything. And it is important also that birds' lives be subjected to scientific inquisitions as to such matters as ergonomics and ecology, because we are ever more responsible for them and need scientific knowledge the better to discharge our obligation as stewards. In this book I have felt free to lift any scientific insight I have come across with or without attribution, science being *pro bono publica.*

There are yet other ways to look in on the lives of birds. Sometimes it seems sufficient to look no further than the surface and merely follow the delicate tracery of color and movement they provide us – an endless series of anecdotes. You don't have to understand the details of an exotic culture to respect it, or to find it beautiful and comforting. Birds help punctuate our lives even when we don't really know what they are up to. An unpunctuated life is not worth living, is what I say.

For example, there are several birds in my house as I write this. One is a chicken with her chick. She is a Polish hen with a frondy tassle of copper and black feathers on top of her head that makes her look alternately elegant and foolish, like one of those androgynous rock stars. The chick is black and cute as are all baby chickens, and when it peeps, the hen peers angularly at it, topknot swaying, a bebopping guardian. They live in a box in the downstairs bathroom for now because the potential for predation in the chicken house is too great for my wife Susanne to contemplate. There are possums, raccoons, possibly even a fox out there, and the occasional rat as well. Anyway, until the chick is adjudged (by criteria I have yet to hear) grown up enough to take its chances with the other chickens, guests are encouraged to be continent.

Another of the birds here is a parrot whom we used to own lock, stock, and all that when we lived in the city, but out here in the country he took (maybe she took, nobody knows) to shrieking for hours at a time, and after a while this led to me shrieking back. It is hard to concentrate during a prolonged bout of idiotic shrieking – either the bird's or mine. So it came to pass that the parrot was taken over by various daughters and lived in a series of remarkable urban homes filled with *joi de vivre* until the latest parrot-sitter had to visit Indonesia and returned the parrot to us. It is much subdued, perhaps finding life in the country boring after all that high life in the *barrios* of Washington, D.C. I now fear that a consensus on the part of my wife, daughters, and other power groups in my life may soon emerge to the effect that the parrot should spend the last eighty years of its life here.

Life, and the order one tries to impose on it, is fragile for both birds and humans.

The other birds here are finches, seven of them, the relict population of a once-great finch empire that formerly gained hegemony over an entire room in our house. They are discussed elsewhere in this book.

Birds are a daily matter for me, but this did not start out to be a book about birds. In fact, for a long period in my life I really wasn't especially interested in birds. Then I became interested in Susanne and she was interested in birds and before long, on my first "birding" expedition along the Chesapeake and Ohio Canal in Maryland, I had the astonishing experience of peering through a bush one morning barbarously prior to 6:00 A.M. and seeing, about ten feet away, the first prothonotary warbler I had ever seen. It was a golden orange of angelic intensity – as all birders know, of course – and, thus rewarded with immediate gratification, I soon had a little life-list under way, noting down in the field guide the place and date of each new sighting. Before long I saw a harlequin duck in Esquimault Lagoon near Victoria, British Columbia, and was so amazed I almost fell in the lagoon. The first rose-breasted grosbeak I ever saw was on the Hopi Reservation in northern Arizona where the bird guide explicitly said they didn't occur.

On the other hand, I have no particular intention of deliberately extending my life-list – running off, say, to some remote place because a vagrant Ross' gull has been spotted there. In the first place, all those wretched little peeps look alike to me, and warblers are too damned evasive. Instead, I enjoy whatever birds happen to fly in from the periphery of my vision where, thankfully, they always are these days. Even so, as I said, this book did not start out as a bird book. The thought was to put together some pieces I had written over the past few years on nature and science, as with a previous book of essays, *Pastorale*. What I found out was that, quite often, when I had set out to write about some other subject, birds appeared. And quite often, when I set out to write about a bird, it led into other realms. Once or twice, with iron discipline, I set out to write about a bird and it stayed put until the end.

Some of the material in this book appeared in slightly different form in *Science 83 – 86, Smithsonian, Country, Oceans, National Geographic, Traveler, TDC, Notre Dame, Air & Space,* and the *Washington Post.* I'm grateful to the editors of those publications for the original opportunity they afforded and for their permission to put forth this material again. And I am grateful to a number of other people who opened my eyes to birds and made them a permanent part of my landscape: noninclusively, Susannah Lawrence of Seattle and her outrageous brother, Vint; Eugene Morton of the National Zoo; Tom Lovejoy, once of the World Wildlife Fund and now of the Smithsonian; John Hay of Cape Cod; as well as Joe Browder and R. J. Smith, wherever they are. But mostly, of course, and in the proximate and ultimate sense of the word *gratitude,* Susanne. If it weren't for her, I wouldn't even have a chicken in my house.

Waterford, Virginia

Songs to Birds

A Most Unfortunate Addition?

A FEW DECADES AGO a previous owner tacked a large, boxlike addition to the rear of my house. I have recently discovered that the county records contain, for anyone to see, an official critique of my house by an architectural historian who pronounced it a fine example of the Queen Anne Victorian style, but for its "most unfortunate addition."

Well.

I consider that a most unfortunate pronouncement. The addition is a major benefit for those who live inside the house, providing excellent space for grandchildren and dogs to play downstairs and for a spacious bedroom above. Its walls are mostly windows, and to stand in this unfortunate addition and look west across the pasturelands to the foothills of the Blue Ridge Mountains while a breeze blows smartly through an old spruce in the backyard is akin in feeling to standing at the helm of a great ship putting out to sea. Architectural historians do not care about such things. They are evidently trained to consider people who live in historic houses as imperfect maintenance crews at best, and, at worst, unavoidable pests, parasitizing monuments to a more civil, if inert, past.

The architects will be further discouraged to learn that the addition provides a home for other pests besides my family: starlings. Imperfect carpentry left a small entrance high up on the north wall, and while any number of birds may well have taken advantage of it in the past, it is the starlings who muscled their way in during my watch.

The starling has supporters. Some find it a handsome bird, but I don't. The metallic purple and green sheen they sport reminds me of nothing but a grubby oil slick in a roadside puddle. Their tails are stubby and out of proportion (you don't need a degree in architecture to know a little bit about proportion). It is a shame that someone long ago found the white spots on their oily plumage reminiscent of tiny stars, hence the bird's nearly sacrilegious name. Stars? The way they swagger around the lawn reminds me more of the large and ill-bred bullies of an otherwise happy childhood. But starlings, like bullies everywhere, inspire awe.

Officially they are called European starlings, with a fitting scientific name: *Sturnus vulgaris.* They are among the most successful birds in the world. There are an estimated six hundred million of them on the globe, of which one-third inhabit North America. The United States is home to about three starlings for every house cat. A century ago there were no starlings here; like most of us, they are recent immigrants. In 1880, a lunatic (we can now say for certain) named Eugene Schiefflin brought eighty of the birds to this country from England and, on March 6, released them in New York's Central Park. He released forty more in April. There is a rumor that Schiefflin had devised a crazed scheme to introduce into this country all the birds mentioned in Shakespeare. There is also speculation that, ironically, all or most of the birds spent that first winter roosting in the eaves of the American Museum of Natural History. It *is* documented, most certainly, that one pair nested there the next spring, much to that great institution's lasting embarrassment. The birds took hold. In 1891, twenty starlings had made it to Staten Island. By 1896 they were in Brooklyn, and two years later they were on their way in all directions, reaching Stamford, Connecticut, and moving north up the Hudson as far as Ossining.

Bird people began to look upon the starling with the same wariness that the American Indians no doubt observed the pilgrims. In 1917, ornithologist Edward Howe Forbush wrote: "As undesirable qualities are often accentuated when a bird is introduced into a new country, we cannot view the introduction of the Starling without some apprehension." Pointing to the bird's "general fitness for the battle of life," Forbush insightfully pointed out that the starling thrives especially in cultivated lands and that in Europe it had had thousands of years to adapt to such places, as well as to the propinquity of large numbers of people, while the native American songbirds, with whom the starling was already seen to be competing, had had only a couple of centuries of such learning conditions. Bird people already knew that the likes of wrens, bluebirds, flickers – virtually any bird that nested in a hole big enough for a starling – would have to step aside. The starling was reported, for example, to lurk around while a flicker patiently crafted a nest hole, and then to appropriate it. After a minor struggle, the flicker would go off to build another nest, only to have it appropriated by yet another starling.

By 1953, Rex Stout had devised a recipe for eating starlings in polenta sauce. By his account Nero Wolfe, the overweight gourmand and detective, was served this dish without sage and quite properly sent it back to the kitchen.

By 1959, the same year that Alaska was admitted to the Union, there were starlings in San Diego: manifest destiny for starlings, achieved in a mere sixty-nine years. Today, from southeastern Alaska to northern Mexico, there is hardly a place they do not inhabit, even the beach. They are often found in the company of grackles, blackbirds, and other lowlifes. In March, hundreds, even thousands, of members of this demimonde gather in the skeletal trees around my house and in the pasture, jostling and shrieking. They suddenly gust up and swarm in the air like insects, only to settle down in other trees nearby, continuing their unmusical chorus. The racket is awesome, the sheer numbers ominous. When "the bad folk all get together," as country singer Jim Croce once put it, there is usually trouble in store.

Some experts say that starlings actually provide great benefit from an economic standpoint. The chief enemy of the clover weevil, they also serve to control cutworms and Japanese beetles. Half their diet consists of insects of one sort or another, mostly ground-dwelling insects, but they will pick off the occasional wasp or bee as well. Thus, they are said to be the farmer's friend. But at any given moment, you can have too many friends around. When a flock of starlings, sometimes numbering in the tens of thousands, swarms into a cherry orchard or vineyard and methodically takes the entire season's fruit crop, the farmer or vintner would probably prefer the mercies of a few enemies. In fact, starlings have become major pests in wheat fields and sunflower plots (thus messing up songbirds from two directions) as well as cherry orchards, and they rapaciously steal cattle feed from any open trough. Around here, the local starlings gorge on my chickens' laying mash, a feed designed to promote fecundity of all things.

Certainly starlings do little to improve the quality of life in the cities and towns they frequent. For several years, for example, beginning in the spring of 1979, a gigantic roost struck a park in Leicester, England. Perhaps a million birds took up nightly residence. Their droppings ruined picnic tables, turned paths into malodorous, slippery hazards, and produced an acidic effect in the soil that killed off many of the park's plants and shrubs. Branches were even broken off trees. Each day at dawn, the birds would begin to twitter, this soon rising to a nearly deafening crescendo at which point wave after wave of starlings – spaced about two or three minutes apart – would rise up like dark clouds of smoke, taking specific flight lines out of the city to various distant feeding grounds. After a day's foraging, they formed up at what British ornithologists identified, with a kind of military fatalism, as twenty outlying "pre-roost assembly points," from which they then descended again upon the hapless park. As they approached, they engaged in astounding aerial maneuvers over the city, leading one observer, Ann Tate, to wonder – as so many have before – about the superb synchronization of their flight, especially since they appear to be leaderless. "Thousands of birds swept and soared, stunt-riding the sky," she wrote. "At invisible signals they dropped into the trees, then rose again to stream upwards, circle and resettle. The noise was immense. What is the purpose of it all?"

God's wrath? Scientists do not believe in such things, but they don't know the purpose of it all either. The birds are obviously expending a great deal of energy in these aerial displays, and such enormous air shows can and often do attract predators like hawks from far and wide. When a predator shows up, the streaming, soaring starlings instantaneously merge into tighter, dark balls too dense to allow penetration. It would appear that there is some sort of communication during these spectaculars aside from alarm calls at the sight of predators: Ms. Tate speculated (perhaps a bit wildly) that maybe in all that apparent chaos there is a system, like the dance of the bees, for learning from one another about the locations for the best food. It is a Hitchcockian thought and, I hope, not the case.

In any event, once such a group settles down for the night, there is a lot of jostling and bickering. Like seagulls, starlings require each other's company but are nonetheless grumpy about it. The nightly squabbles and shoving matches concern position. They all evidently want to be in the core of the roost since it provides better protection from nocturnal predators as well as warmth on cold nights. Generally speaking, the core is inhabited by older, large male bullies with smaller, younger females relegated to the edge. It is not known if the big old males play some leadership role, such as guiding the successive starling waves that head out to forage in the morning.

However starling society works, close observers use such phrases as "highly organized" and "supremely adaptable and efficient" to describe it. Here is something like an army, one that has so far defied the human imagination when it comes to getting rid of it. The FAA stands help-less when starlings are slurped up into the engines of large jet aircraft. There may be a lesson about hubris here, but hubris is not on the FAA's agenda. Starlings are not fooled by tape recordings of their dis-tress signals and are undaunted by bright lights, explosions, dog packs, water hoses, flares. There is no suitable starlicide either. One current strategy is to take advantage of the starling's ability to learn. The search is on for a chemical deterrent, something that would be sufficiently toxic that the starlings, having once or twice been made to feel awful, would quickly learn to avoid anything that tasted or looked like what they had eaten. So wary are the birds that if one gets sick it will thereaf-ter avoid any unaffected companions that happened to be around at the time. Leading candidates in the chemical search are tannins, sub-stances with an astringent effect produced in many plants (tea, for ex-ample) as natural defenses against herbivores. The clue arises from the observation that species of sunflowers relatively high in tannins are the least likely to lose their seeds to starlings.

So farmers await clinical trials of tannins and related substances that they can spray around the place and send the starlings off to . . . where? Some other farm? Meanwhile I am placing my bets on the starlings, much as I hate to. Starlings are simply too good at what they do to be pushed around for long. They seem smart. It is not clear that mimicry is related to intelligence among birds, for example, but it may be. And the starling is an underrated mimic, pulling off the songs of virtually every bird that frequents my yard, as well as a wolf whistle they may have picked up from the parrot and passed along from generation to generation. Starlings have been known to imitate dog barks, the sounds of machinery, even the ringing of the telephone. A college pro-fessor is reported to have taught a captive starling to say "*Sturnus vulgaris*" as confidently as any ornithologist. It *is* amusing to listen to these vaguely sleazy upstarts imitate their social superiors – cardinals, robins, and the rest of what might be thought of here in Virginia as

First Families. Intelligence or no, starlings have a distinct series of legs up on the other songbirds when it comes to survival.

First, they are stronger and more muscular than other birds their size, with skulls and necks built much like a woodpecker's. Their aggression, even among themselves, is well known. I once stood transfixed as two starlings wrassled and slashed each other for more than twenty minutes, rolling around the lawn, shrieking in what looked like mortal combat, till one of them wobbled off, leaving the other panting on the grass.

Second, their yellow beaks are very sharp but, more than that, operate in a way unique among insect-hunting birds. Most birds can exert a surprising amount of force when they close their mandibles; a starling can also exert a great force when it *opens* its beak. This in itself makes it especially good at foraging for insects and worms under the soil, allowing it to open up a two-inch gash in the lawn to find its prey.

Third, a special visual capacity evolved along with the starling's useful beak. Behind the beak, the skull is quite narrow, which means that the eyes emerge at an angle that provides more forward vision than in most birds. Further, the starling can move its eyes – together or independently – forward, backward, and upward. The bird can thus attain about forty-five degrees of binocular vision in front of him, almost equaling the owl's capacity. And thanks to a peculiar configuration of the starling's retina and other structures of the inner eye, it is both myopic and farsighted at the same time. Having myopic binocular vision means that the bird can focus on the region near the tip of its bill, making perusal for subsoil prey more efficient. Nor does it need to pause and cock its head to see what it has turned up, as other birds must. (The way birds cock their heads is somehow – to me – endearing: perhaps the fact that starlings don't do this makes them a bit creepy, even menacing.) At the same time, thanks to the starling eye's internal asymmetry, the outer regions of the retina are farsighted. So, while looking with sharp, nearsighted binocular vision at what's going on around its prying beak, the bird can – without pausing even for the instant it takes you or me to refocus our eyes – simultaneously be on the lookout for distant predators. Such efficient vision lets the bird find food where and when other birds can't, and this in turn makes it relatively easy for the starling to raise two, sometimes three, broods of young each season, going forth and multiplying with a vigor and determination that would amaze the authors of biblical edicts.

Which brings me back to the starlings that live in the wall of my unfortunate addition. I sense an unspoken, even nonspecific community pressure to seal up the hole and rid the house of these tagalongs. To shut them off I would, in all fairness, have to wait until all the young were gone, but each year, once their squalling ceases, I forget, remembering only in the spring when once again it is too late for evictions. Life, my muse tells me, generally outlasts architecture: there's a rule of thumb for you. Also, the birds don't seem to be enlarging the hole or doing any structural damage. (And even if they were, causing the addition to fall off before long, the architects would surely applaud.) If I evict these starlings, they will simply evict some flicker. There are sanitary conditions to consider – vermin and all. Ever efficient, starlings tend to return year after year and reuse the old nest. Why waste time? But after several seasons, nests get pretty pest-ridden. But starlings are personally fastidious. They bathe a lot, preen a lot, even try to keep their feet from getting muddy. Prissy bullies. And each spring in March and April, the males do a bit of restoration on their historic homes. They weave the tips of young plant shoots into the old nest. Scientists have found that the birds prefer nine particular plants for this task and all nine of them contain a variety of chemicals that act as natural fumigants. Some drive bacteria and other parasites away, others act like hormones to inhibit the hatching of eggs of pests such as lice.

Awesome indeed: starlings long ago completed their chemical research and clinical trials. Surely they are with us for the duration, analogues to remind us of our own record here on a once-virgin continent. The starlings will probably stay in the house. I still don't like them, mind you. I don't like their swagger, and when a parent flies on a javelin-straight trajectory from the pasture to the hole in my house, it reminds me of nothing so much as a stubby, dark, low-flying warplane. I've got to hand it to starlings for their many talents in the battle for life, but I won't take my hat off to them.

The Pond

No matter what else may be going on behind my house – in the trees, in the pasture, the hills beyond, the sky – the pond always draws my eyes in a subconscious sweep, a proprietor's glance. There are no natural ponds in this region, the Piedmont, which means the foot of the hills. I live in the foot of the foothills, the essence of landscape humility.

There are a number of geological reasons why there are no ponds around here. Some have to do with the fact that water runs well downhill, others to do with soil impermeability, yet others with the inability of the last glacier to make it this far south. But it is by no means inappropriate to use a bulldozer or other means to *create* ponds in this area. Ponds are quite benign additions, found on farms, estates, in backyards, even in the middle of towns. They attract geese, which can't hurt a land. In flusher days the United States Department of Agriculture encouraged, even helped finance, the building of farm ponds around this region.

Such high-rolling bureaucrats would have sniffed at our pond because it is really more puddle than pond. It is only about twelve feet long, some seven feet across, and three feet deep at one end. I suspect it would have been bigger, or smaller, depending on the attention span and the energy of the Head Landscape Architect here who, one hot day, simply started digging a hole in the backyard. In fairness, maybe she dug until she had achieved the precise configuration dictated by her own sense of esthetics. In any event, there was then a hole in the clayey (and unattractive) soil in the backyard, right on the edge where the lawn meets what we call "the wild area," a small patch of yard left to be field, wildflowers, raspberries, and pretty much whatever it determines on its own. To this day, it is impossible to say whether the pond is an extension of the lawn, a relatively manicured place, or of the wild area. (We will not allow trees to get started in the wild area: this is a yard in a rural town, not a wilderness.) Maybe the pond is a link between them, a conjunction like the word *and.*

But first it was a hole in the ground, unsightly and full of omens for me, chiefly presaging a great deal of work, the details of which I could not imagine and the magnitude of which I dreaded.

There had been little discussion of this pond before the hole was dug. A good idea, we had agreed, and I went on to other things. Good ideas abound here. Some take on a material reality; others simply float like comfortable ghosts, an optimistic cloudscape of potentialities that are in some ways as important to making a place a home as actually building bookshelves and planting rows of tomatoes. Then, my wife somehow took hold of the idea and, selecting it from among the many wraiths of possibilities, dug the hole, which gaped at me ominously for a week or two.

Fortunately, my wife and I have raised many daughters. Daughters tend to attract swains, and swains are often of more use than sons, for they have a direct interest in pleasing everyone involved. One such fellow arrived one day, enlisted me as a hod carrier, and we built the cement shell in the hole that became the pond. We cured it, circled its edge with rock liberated from a stone wall, and filled it with water. We later discovered that it leaked ever so slightly but by then it was too late for repairs. Things were already living in it, aquatic things that no one had the heart to disrupt, so we simply took to adding water to the pond daily. No swain is perfect.

But perfection is a kind of mental tyranny, isn't it? It exists nowhere in nature, except perhaps for perfect musical pitch. The pond, we hoped, would suffice, although we didn't know what that meant, either.

For any proprietor of a new pond, there are two strategies open. The first: do nothing and let nature take its course. The second: intervene and then let nature take its course, which it always does. Both strategies are laden with uncertainty piled upon uncertainty. Now, uncertainty is a state which the physicists find common throughout the universe but one which the human brain, left to itself and momentarily free of the dismaying assertions of physicists, finds offensive. Human brains are not designed for ambiguity. For example, from the time light reflected from some object like a pond hits the eye's retina to the time when an image ultimately takes shape in the mind, millions of specialized cells found in a host of regions in the brain pick, choose, modify, and refine the data. It is our neurons that produce a concise message out of what is evidently the blur of reality and provide us with an edited version that satisfies the human sense of how things should be. The brain is thus, structurally, a moralist, and that may be why people often fret over the notion of perfection. The point here is that the infamous scale of one-to-ten applies to nothing in the world and certainly not the pond behind my house. The pond would be better if it didn't leak, I grant you, but so would governments, plumbing, old people, and ozone layers. I'm interested in the *aptness* of ponds, not engineering procedures.

Montaigne said that one must be ignorant of many things in order to act and so, when faced with the crystalline water of our new pond, we intervened. We couldn't imagine how water lilies and fish would get to the pond without our help, and a backyard pond without them does, after all, seem aimless. So, for about the same amount we had paid for concrete, we bought two water lilies and one other aquatic plant that looks like an exuberant four-leaf clover. These plants, encased in black plastic buckets, slipped into the depths like ancient and mysterious snapping turtles, giving a muddy cast to the water. Within days, they bloomed. The next issue was fish. We had no idea how hospitable our pond really was – for all I know they put carcinogenic preservatives in concrete mix as routinely as in bacon – so it seemed a bit risky to splurge on some expensive Japanese carp called *koi*, which are *the* thing for upwardly mobile backyard ponds. Instead, for two dollars, we bought twenty "feeder fish," which is to say goldfish bred to be sacrificed to pet alligators, aging Princetonians, or heaven knows what. The thought that we had given these twenty goldfish an entirely new lease on life, a chance at a Pinochioan freedom, was no little comfort.

We then discussed suspending any further intervention to see what sort of aquatic world might arise on its own, five hundred yards from the nearest pond and a thousand yards from the nearest creek. A properly passive sort of scientific experiment, I thought. But the matter was resolved by the appearance of a ten-year-old boy who would often be seen in earnest contemplation of the pond, and who then carried on long discussions at its edge with my wife. I would see them making gentle and graceful hand gestures over the water, two tow-headed shamans cooking something up. The boy, a neighbor's kid named Michael, was dispatched to the creek with a bucket and returned with it full of brownish green water – a single bucket worth a small universe, it turned out.

Within days grotesque little larval forms could be seen squiggling in our shadowy water, tiny bits of energetic threads. Little dark eyes embedded in silvery slivers of gelatin heralded minnows.

As the spring became summer, some nasty-looking monsters with awful hooked jaws became mayflies with graceful, long, feathery tail appendages. Whirligig beetles did their dervish dance; long-legged water striders zipped back and forth, each foot making a nearly microscopic indentation in the water's surface tension. The little dents in the water magnified into luminous circles where the water strider casts its shadow in the shallower end and, as is the case also in many a philosophical discussion ever since Plato's time, it is more fun to watch these light-enhanced shadows on the bottom – here, boink, there, boink, here. . . . Tiny red mites, spider relatives, appeared and disappeared, twinkling in the sunlight. The minnows grew to a couple of inches in length and lurked calmly in the caverns of algae that had grown below the lily pads, coexisting with the goldfish. Some wild strawberry shoots leaned out over the water and soon sent additional roots downward into the murk, hedging their bets or perhaps simply showing off. One would see a metallic blue dragonfly helicoptering among the lilies, hovering and darting on its predatory mission. From one bucket more had arisen, almost, than any shaman could have asked.

But lily pads have always demanded frogs and there were none that anyone had seen – no tadpoles wiggling like frantic sperm under the microscope, no late afternoon croaks, nothing. Then one day, we heard it, a sound like someone plucking a loose banjo string. A frog had appeared and was immediately spotted staring grumpily out from among the pads. It seemed like a case of spontaneous generation.

The Navajo Indians believe that frogs are born of raindrops; after all, out in the desert lands they inhabit there aren't many ponds that last for more than a few days at a time. But after a rain, Navajos soon spot frogs in puddles. So . . . rain drops make frogs. In fact, the frogs of the Southwest desert have miraculously short growth and development schedules, tuned to the waywardness of the climate. In a matter of days, a frog egg becomes a tadpole, then a frog, then mates and then lays eggs that are insulated against aridity and can simply sit there in the dust, to be activated by the next rain. So rain drops *do* make frogs. When it comes to desert frogs, the big picture is really the same for Navajos and biologists.

Our frog was a green frog, not uncommon at all in the East. The banjo call was a giveaway. Many green frogs are really brown but this one was green, with a cheerful bright yellow throat that filled up and emptied with an abrupt heave each time it plucked its banjo string.

Behind its ears it had circular markings (called tympani) that were larger than its eyes and so we knew (thanks to the Peterson guide) that it was a male. How it arrived, we have never found out. It could have come as a tadpole in the bucket and lived its preadult life in total obscurity in the pond. I like the thought that even so small a pond as ours can provide total secrecy for something as noticeable as a growing frog. Or it could have jumped across the pasture and through the hedgerow from the larger and older pond five hundred yards away, like the pilgrims seeking the New World or at least a place less frequented by bossy male green frogs. Or Michael could have caught it from somewhere and donated it without saying so. Any route will do, even the Navajo route, as far as I am concerned. Ponds make frogs.

The green frog remained, sometimes visible and sometimes not, always lending his voice to the chorus at dusk during which time the birds chitter and twit as they settle down. But the frog was not settling down. He was engaged in the sessile cruising of amphibious males seeking sex, and this soon led to another meeting of the shamans. Over the weeks, other green frogs were hauled out of their territories and placed in the pond; they were all males, too, it seems, and fled from the original pilgrim, in one case after what we thought might be a mating ritual involving a lot of leaping and chasing but turned out to be an outright fight. The frog is still, to this day, celibate. He has survived two winters, as have the lilies, the fish, and the rest. He did have a brief time as a voyeur but there is no way of telling if this satisfied him or merely sharpened his longings.

We had noticed toads around the place, dark khaki-colored American toads. One day, on the edge of the pond under an overhanging rock in the shade of the wild area, we noticed two toads mating, the smaller male sitting burgherlike on top of the equally expressionless female. From what we could make out, toad sex is less exciting than watching water erode a mountain. Nothing moved; the stolid, even statuesque stillness of toad passion exceeded our attention span. We came and went through the morning, occasionally checking to see if they were still at it. But the green frog's attention span works on a different wave length than ours and one that is no doubt closer to the toads'. All day, the frog lay motionless in the water about a foot away, directly in front of the amorous toads, only his head above the surface. It was late in the afternoon, at a time when we were away, that the cameo dissolved. Whatever was the climax, and my guess is that it would have been imperceptible to us, the toads were gone, and so was the frog.

It is said that the nerve cells of the frog are structured in such a way that, from the great blur of reality, they only pick up little dark spots in motion. Even a motionless dark spot doesn't register electrically as anything special in the frog brain. In the relatively fragile world of being a frog, it must pay to notice only moving things. Thus, reality in frogs is a flying insect or maybe the shadow of a ten-year-old boy. But I'd be willing to bet that if neuroscientists looked again, they would find some nerve cells in frogs that let them know that something is up among toads, as motionless as such affairs are.

Before long the pond was filled with hundreds, indeed thousands, of little dark tadpoles, thrashing their tails in chaos and hugging the (perhaps warmer) sides of the pond. For several weeks they remained; the shallow sides of the pond were darkened with them, so many it struck me as oddly ominous. And then one day they were all toads, hundreds and hundreds of little toads no bigger than houseflies, complete with forelegs and back legs. And in the alarming numerical extravagance of toad reproduction, these minitoads seemed less scary than the horde of tadpoles had.

Also tastier, in some quarters. Robins would deign to leave the greensward and pick off a few brown minitoads, whisking them out of the shallows like hors d'oeuvres. Over the days there was noticeable attrition but hundreds still remained. It was a severe dry spell, and hot. My wife noticed that many, as they eventually sought to make the exodus from water across the cement and rocks to the lawn, would dehydrate on the spot and die. This was not something that would ever happen in a natural pond, so yet more intervention was justified. She removed voluminous tresses of green algae from the pond and festooned the edges with them, also allowing the hose to drip into the algae to keep it moist. The next day all the toads were gone, off to adventure with a destiny that includes even lawnmowers. There is practically no wilderness left.

But even as man-made a thing as that little pond is, it retains a certain amount of independence, a certain amount of its own dialectic. In winter it freezes over and what survives (which is a lot) does so without any help on our part. Even in winter it can become a source of excitement. Early one November morning, after a flock of yellow grosbeaks had blown into the neighborhood like a gaudy motorcycle gang, leaving the proletarian sparrows and house finches that hang out at the bird feeder in obvious amazement, I saw a few of the newcomers standing on the water of the pond. During a night that had brought a light frost, the surface of the pond had frozen just enough to support their weight; they hopped around on the ice in their yellow and black uniforms, exhibitionists, and then all gusted up and headed south. Minutes later the pond's surface had turned to liquid. Timing is everything in show business.

There has been mortality, of course, beyond the daily loss of insect life and the robins' raids on innocent toadlets. (I happen not to be especially fond of robins, a sacrilegious position perhaps, but I have my reasons.) And one day, there was a moment of terror on the part of us pond proprietors when it became clear that a snake was swimming in there, a garter snake. The minnows were doomed. The instinct was to remove the interloper. But an even more primal sense took over – the simple awe engendered by any charismatic predator. So we watched the snake perform in dominant ess-curves for a while, and it left. If it caught a minnow (or even if it wanted a minnow) we don't know.

Aside from the frog, a stately character even if he is essentially dim-witted, the creature we were fondest of was a small turtle, a slider imported by Michael. It enjoyed the pond as much as anyone, clearly finding life in even so tiny a wildlife refuge nevertheless a pleasant existence. It roamed, and nibbled algae, and hunted little creatures, and sunned itself on lily pads, and peered from the murk, and even ate from my wife's fingers. Then one day we found it dead, lying between the water and the rocks on the concrete. Just like that. Cause unknown. Turtles are probably the least understandable of all creatures; that may be what recommends them so.

In such ways are we the gods – well, maybe angels – of the little pond, establishing it as an Eden of lilies and goldfish in the first place, bringing in the mythological Great Bucket of Life from which so much evidently flowed, tending, fretting, maintaining the water supply, sitting back and admiring it on sabbathlike occasions, admitting the pond and its creatures into our dreams, watching the sky reflected from its surface in the afternoon, pink and orange with the sunset, and imagining that in some way here in this tiny body of water staring up at the sky is an infinitesimal nerve cell of God's eye, conjoining heaven and earth. And why not? There is really nothing wrong with such thoughts as long as they don't get beyond the limits of a proper humility. I don't really know much about ponds when it comes down to it. I have never lived in or on ponds: my brain cells are more attuned to linguistical affairs than gurgles, more to engineering projects than caverns of algae.

But our pond has actually been certified by a creature that knows as much about such places as anyone will ever need to know. One afternoon, my wife called excitedly for me to come outside on the back porch. When I got there, she pointed upwards and said "Look, look at that!" An osprey was overhead. It is also known as a fish hawk, but is more properly thought of as a fish eagle as far as I'm concerned, because it is a lordly bird. Ospreys are generally found around bays and rivers (where fish are) and they have evidently begun to reextend their range in these slightly more enlightened times. There are some to be found on the upper reaches of the Potomac River, about ten miles from here, and every so often one wanders this far inland. The osprey is big and somehow ghostly, and when it is not soaring on thermals with wings outstretched, it flies almost languorously with what Audubon called "easy flappings," as much an owner of the air and the water as any bald eagle.

This one was flying fairly low over the pasture, as if on some routine reconnaissance, when it turned, descended a bit, and circled the pond three times. Then it resumed its way south. The pond, our pond, had been noted by an osprey. It was now part of an osprey's map of the world – a pond to be reckoned with, by god.

Bird Lists and Junk Mail

IT WASN'T JUST the bird feeder's fault. I've ordered a lot of things from catalogs and direct mail appeals, even a United States president who never made it, despite my generosity. Once I ordered a set of small woodcarver's chisels, a bench knife, and a pair of powerful magnifying glasses that clip onto my own glasses, with a view to making a tidy fortune on the side by carving two-inch-long duck decoys out of basswood. No fortune resulted, but I know in my fingers a lot more about the nature of bird anatomy, and I am now the recipient of every tool catalog in the world, including a West Coast salvage company that once a month tries to persuade me to buy a gigantic World War II surplus band saw for cutting tanks into useful slabs. Originally, I ordered the bird feeder – the kind with clear plastic suction cups that stick right on the windowpane and, later, a hanging feeder surrounded with wire mesh to discourage squirrels – and now I am the daily recipient of messages from any organization that believes there is a chance that I, a feeder of birds, share an interest in their product: flowers and seeds, bird books, style magazines, conservation, optic and camping equipment, land deals, group tours of parasite-infested regions, celebrations of Arbor Day, you name it. I am for rent. I have learned that my name and address are worth approximately a nickel out there on the direct mail block. Don't laugh. That's about what yours is worth too.

Some people object to junk mail strenuously. They find it an intrusion into the perfect order of their lives, possibly unconstitutional, and apparently more malign than the invasion by someone on a street – or a beach – with a hundred-pound transmitter of the screeches and moans that our youth take to be music.

I think junk mail is nifty. And I am sure Audubon would have hustled his books by junk mail if he had ever heard of it. And why not? Out here in what Bloomingdale's thinks of as the boondocks, I can't keep up easily with the centers of fashion and commerce – they don't change models each year down at the local chicken feed store, a cooperative called Southern States. So I rely on the people who rent my name and address to each other to help me keep up with a rapidly changing world.

Some people who complain about junk mail have probably been brought up in the puritanical tradition of chicken economics and marketing: one egg, properly managed, will make another chicken. Direct mail marketing, on the other hand, is based on the principle of fish reproduction – a seemingly scandalous profusion of eggs cast loose in the waters, all to provide at best a handful of surviving fish. It seems profligate but it has worked perfectly well for fish for several hundred million years, and it works tolerably well for direct mail marketers as well. It takes only a handful of orders for every hundred pieces of junk mail sent out to create a success: a five percent response is more than enough to make the mailer weep in joyous fulfillment.

You have probably had this effect on such people yourself. If you have one of those suction-cup bird feeders, you know all this already. More than likely you have been found by a magazine because you had earlier bought something else by direct mail – another magazine, an expensive sleeping bag, whatever. And you were thereby known to be a reliable citizen.

Suppose your name was in the computer of the Phillips Screwdriver and Carriage Company, because you ordered several screwdrivers and, more recently, an Italian harness for your carriage horse. What is important is that they discovered you actually *paid* for such things, as most people do. Had you not paid and needed to be ceaselessly dunned by an astonishingly rude and persistent collection agency, you would have become what is known in the trade as a "bad debt." This information would stick to you like a lamprey and you would, in later trades of names from Phillips to the Friends of the Earth or the Committee to Arm the Third World, be personally and electronically "merged and purged" (as the industry has it), probably never again to be given the privilege of making a bid on a piece of underwater estate.

Of course, there *are* mountebanks in the direct mail business, just as there are mountebanks in every medium, and if you suspect you're being defrauded by mail, your postmaster is obliged to help you raise civic hell. Or if you don't like the idea of your name becoming a commercial commodity you can instruct a junk mailer to bloody well keep your name to himself. Before long you will be merged and purged, of course, into total oblivion – which I don't recommend.

I really like the idea of so simple a system as junk mail. It *is* direct, usually unambiguous, and sometimes surprising. At my end it is passive. It doesn't ring at dinnertime like telephone solicitations (my notion of a capital crime), but beckons my attention merely by the artfulness of the presentation on an otherwise inert envelope. With some fraction of the day's envelopes opened (others not), I still retain the option to register no in private. And I've got to take out the trash in any case. Junk mailers usually avoid excess weight because they pay by weight, so I can't seriously complain about even the unappealing junk mail. It is harmless.

But mainly I like the idea that so many of the great engines of industry consider me – even though I live in a place of total insignificance – still the sort of fellow who can in so many ways join in the high-tech enterprise of our culture. It is democratic in a sense that would please

Jefferson, who would also have applauded the role of the Sears catalog in civilizing the American frontier.

I am free to fantasize about (or even obtain) a handcrafted Finnish pukka knife to open up my hundred-pound sacks of chicken feed. I could elect to consult a digital weather system embedded in a leather swivel chair complete with heat-activated switches to load and start the dishwasher. Do I want Florida grapefruit? Two hundred pounds of sunflower seeds (already husked for the little dears)? All this is mine for the asking.

But there is a non-Jeffersonian elitism creeping into the junk mail business. People with the idea of selling leather-backed weather stations or Audubon's peeps printed on rice paper in eight (8) colors, or china sets featuring George Washington's greatest moments, are looking for "up-scale" lists of names, and so a certain egalitarianism is being lost. The perfect up-scale family, as I hear it, has at least one forty-two-year-old adult well launched on a career trajectory that has just about reached senior partner or the professional or managerial equivalent. Two cars are essential and someone in the family must have been to graduate school for at least 1.1 years. They should have 2.3 children, at least half of whom are accepted at Princeton, several sound systems, two personal computers, a VCR, and what is evidently referred to as a videocam, which entitles people with no sense of story to make immediately viewable epics of Freddie learning the art of toilet training.

As the science – at least the statistical science – of what is called demographics becomes more intimately entwined with marketing, it is probably inevitable that even finer distinctions will be made among us citizens. And, alas, the mailboxes of those who are not deemed up-scale will become embarrassingly barren. Dreams will go unstimulated. And if you fall off the list of the up-scale, you will miss the most amusing part of all: tracking your name through the labyrinths of corporate America, a sociological study in its own right, as well as pondering how you (if you're male) somehow got your first name feminized by some series of computer glitches and soon learned more about the needs of women than you might even think it proper to know. (In the mists of earlier, less-advanced microcircuitry, my dog managed to get on the mailing list of a ball-point pen manufacturer in Florida – a very down-scale item, I fear, though looked at from the economic status of dogs, who is to say?)

Now how do the captains of industry know you are up-scale? Partly because your name is already on the consumer lists of people who sell up-scale items. But this is vague, full of potential ambiguities. Someone might own an Alfa Romeo but secretly prefer American beer to imported wine, a serious demographic character flaw. Or one may eschew a $2,000 word processor in favor of a $45 fountain pen and a brain. Yet more ambiguity: a fountain pen is relatively up-scale compared to a ball-point accidentally liberated from the dry-cleaners' or even bought in bulk from Florida by a dog.

The better to penetrate this cloud-cover of variables, direct marketeers, like magazine publishers, will occasionally send out questionnaires to randomly selected ("*n*th name") collections of people on their list, often with a dollar bill or other inducement enclosed which, when pocketed, morally obliges the recipient to answer. Such questionnaires often begin inanely enough with a query about how much did you enjoy, say, our last issue? (Very much, a lot, not much, and other precision-type indices.) Next, subtly, they will ask which article you enjoyed most. Answer from memory, picking an article that was actually published in another magazine, and *your* response becomes junk mail on the spot.

What the questioner really wants to know comes later. Next is your income. You can check "$15,000–$24,000" and on up perhaps to the stately "More than $100,000." You must report your travel plans, your reading *and* book buying habits (the two being separable and the world evidently being littered with unread books), how many stereos, birding scopes, and pianos you possess and all that. Of course the questionnaire is almost saccharine in its amicability and also anonymous, so you are encouraged to be honest, but just who would confess to less than $15,000 a year, no credit cards, and no stereo, even anonymously, is beyond me.

At any rate, this is all more or less innocent, if demanding of private and potentially embarrassing mid-career self-evaluation. But you are then asked your age and here is where things get insidious, for it is this datum that the marketeers truly want.

The marketeer needs to know if you are 20–29, 30–39, or 40–49. The latter, as I've said, renders you of heroic proportion. Then there is a box that more often than not is labelled 50–89. There is no difference made between a fifty-one-year-old just hitting what he or she foolishly imagines to be stride and a toothless, tottering octogenarian. Anyone in this large age-caste is presumed beyond benefit of a management consultant and untrainable in the new tricks of recovery-style consumerism. Any old crock of fifty or more is clearly too set in his or her ways to find a pressing need for a Danish lemon peeler with a digital egg-timer set in its rosewood handle. Such folk may well wobble off and buy a Mercedes in some pathetic final burst of glory, but they'll drive it at forty miles per hour or less in third gear and keep the damn thing a decade and are thus of no interest whatsoever to up-scale auto merchandisers, never mind constructors of ORVs.

Lately that final demographic box beckoned icily in my direction. I had to make the choice. I could knowingly demarcate myself as demographically inconsequential. Or I could lie and be, eternally, 40–49.

I lied.

Every year I'll buy some useless solar-powered coat hanger from the Sharper Image catalog and a jade toothpick from Gump's and each Christmas I will requisition by mail some flimsy, slightly naughty trifle of lingerie from the folks at Victoria's Secret and baffle the new sociologists of commerce while astounding my wife (also eternally 40–49), and that way no one will ever notice that I am moribund.

Deceit

SEAGULLS LIE.

Seagulls are social though not sociable, and querulous to a fault, but they wouldn't seem smart enough to prevaricate. Yet they have been caught doing just that by Eugene Morton, who is an ornithologist at the National Zoo, and this, along with a great deal of new research, is casting a new light on the old question: do animals think?

Morton, who is as close as we have come to a scientific Dr. Dolittle, has found that all animals share a kind of grammar of expression which he calls "expressive sound symbols." By these symbolic noises, animals can communicate their feelings of the moment not just among themselves but across species lines.

Throughout the animal world, Morton discovered, angry animals growl; frightened, friendly, or submissive animals whine; and aroused or interested animals bark. While it is hard to imagine a bird barking, it can be seen to do so when its voice is recorded on a sonogram, a two-dimensional acoustic voiceprint often used to record and analyze bird songs. The chirps of a bird and the bark of a dog, for example, have the identical shape of a chevron. Growls – of a wren or a tiger – appear as thick vertical bands.

This universal language (at least among animals with vocal capacities) evidently saves everyone a lot of time and energy. A territorial male can growl and perhaps discourage some intruder without having to fight. Moreover, big animals tend to have lower voices than smaller ones. Thus a small animal making a low sound seems bigger, and vice-versa: a high tonal whine sounds like a smaller animal or a young animal and therefore becomes a sign of appeasement. Once such an insight occurs, it seems obvious, but no one had this insight into animal communication (or at least no one had announced it) until Gene Morton did.

There can be shades of meaning in sound as well. A screech could be a combination of an aggressive growl and the high-pitched whine of fear. And it gets more complicated than that.

For example, a mother goose being attacked by a fox may well have ambivalent feelings, Morton points out. She may be scared half to death and her instinct is to flee. At the same time she is urgently impelled to protect her young. If she emits a vocal sound, it might go either way – high (submission) or low (aggression) or both, but the risk of honest fear erupting forth and the fox reading this accurately is too great. Instead, geese in such situations have come to emit a nonvocal sound. They hiss, which expresses neither emotion. The goose doesn't lie by pretending to be fearless, but she doesn't tell the truth either. On the other hand, the goose's hiss would seem to be part of the circuitry, not a calculated dodge each time.

As for gulls, biologists have noticed that, in a flock, the first one to spot a morsel of food will often but not always emit a high-pitched cry before diving for the food. It is clear that the gull is not being submissive and letting the other bullies get there first. Morton theorizes that the gull emits the high-pitched call to tell the others that it is under attack from some predator. This has the effect of distracting the others, making them hesitate for a split second, and giving the lying – yes, lying – bird the chance to get there first. This is not to knock seagulls for a bit of mendacity. They have fine qualities too. Monogamous, a pair shares egg-sitting duties equally and fairly, an instance of what my wife calls "egullitarianism."

But the idea of animals deceiving one another by what appears to be deliberate manipulation of the meaning of symbols suggests that something at least akin to thought is going on. Certainly it suggests that the gull's brain is capable of more than mere mechanical reactions to outside stimuli. Possibly this is a kind a conscious awareness. (Of course, that the ploy evidently continues to work among gulls time after time suggests a little bit less than what we would call intelligence.)

Similar behavior has been noted among shrikes in the Amazon. Typically, a foraging flock has one member act as sentinel, to warn with a particular alarm call if a hawk approaches. Often, the sentinel sounds the alarm only to beat a flock member to an insect morsel. The other shrikes don't seem to care.

Another example of deceit in the world of birds is to be found among various ground-nesting birds like grouses, killdeers, and other plovers which feign injury – flapping around with what looks like a broken wing – when a potential predator approaches their nests. Some scientists have proposed that this is not an attempt to fool the intruder and lead it away from the nest, but merely a hysterical response on the part of the parent caught between the same emotional Scylla and Charybdis as the mother goose – an automaton's reaction made in a random direction. But Carolyn Ristau of New York's Rockefeller University has been studying plovers' broken wing displays and reports that the plover parent does move in a direction that would lead the intruder away from the nest and, during the maneuver, tunes her behavior to that of the intruder. Also, she reports, the plovers soon learn who is a safe intruder and who isn't. All this suggests that it is deceit and not merely a mechanical response.

Animal behaviorists, as well as philosophers, have typically sought to explain the activities and even apparent group strategies of animals as genetically programmed or as the result of fairly mechanical conditioned responses (a form of learning), which most of them surely are.

Thinking, awareness, and consciousness have largely been denied non-human creatures for many reasons, from the desire to avoid anthropomorphism to the fact that it is simply difficult to ask an animal what it is thinking, if it is thinking at all, or for that matter, what it thinks about being part of a scientific experiment. Recently, however, inspired by a book called *Animal Thinking* by the distinguished zoologist Donald Griffin, also of Rockefeller University, a number of zoologists have opened up the question of thoughtful behavior in the rest of the animal kingdom.

Deliberate deceit has been found nowhere in the animal kingdom so much as among primates. In one flagrant and famous scandal in these circles, a female hamadryas baboon engaged in a clandestine affair with a younger male. Typically in such troops, a dominant male sees to it that the harem remains faithful to him. In this instance, the illicit pair hid from the old boy behind a rock. After each coupling, the female would look up innocently over the rock and, in one instance, went over to the leader and presented herself as available to him, reassuring him that all was well before heading back for more trysting behind the rock.

In another case, among gelada baboons, a philandering pair was out of sight but within earshot of the dominant male. So the cuckolder withheld the loud cries all gelada males make during "honest" matings. It can be argued that this took not just premeditation but uncommon will power.

Vervet monkeys have three different alarm calls for three different predators – eagles, leopards, and snakes. Each elicits the appropriate behavior by the troop. The eagle alarm sends them off to ground cover; the leopard alarm sends them up into the trees. The snake alarm leads them simply to scrutinize the ground nearby. There is something more than automatic about these calls: they are emitted only when the monkeys are in a group, not if the alarmed monkey is alone. Alarm calls from adolescents are normally ignored as likely to be overreactions.

This is an example of what is called third-order intentionality, wherein the signaller conveys that it wants its companions to know something so that they can take the proper action. (First-order intentionality is where I simply want to go indoors. Second-order is when I want to go inside because I want to replenish my julep and I know the fixings are inside.) It is another step up the intentionality scale when vervets falsely use an alarm call to break up a territorial fight that is going poorly for the signaller's side. Deceit, in other words, functions in a situation where the deceiver has an idea what the other guy is probably thinking about or expecting.

Intentionality is what scientists in this realm call a mental state, clearly a prerequisite for thinking. David Premack and his colleagues at the University of California at Berkeley set out some years ago to see if a chimpanzee was able to attribute a mental state to a human being. It was a new wrinkle on earlier studies that had shown that a chimpanzee is smart enough to figure out that, if it makes a platform by piling up two boxes, it can reach some bananas hung otherwise out of reach.

In this instance, Premack showed a chimpanzee a videotape of a human jumping up and down, waving his arms, trying to reach a bunch of bananas overhead. Then the chimp was shown several photographs, most of them utterly irrelevant, one showing two boxes lying around and one showing two boxes piled one on top of the other. (The chimp has never been involved in the reaching-for-the banana gambit, but it *had* been trained that the choice of a situationally relevant photograph would lead to a reward.) The chimp chose the photograph of the boxes piled up.

It is difficult not to conclude that the chimp correctly attributed a mental state, intention, to the human since otherwise the photograph of two boxes piled up would have had no meaning whatsoever. The chimp had to have known that the idiot jumping up and down wanted the bananas, and to have somehow realized that in one of many photographs, the answer was at hand.

In another series of experiments, Premack looked at the chimpanzee's ability to deliberately deceive. A chimp named Sadie was allowed to get to know two trainers – one, she learned, was a "good guy," the other a "bad guy." The good guy would share food with Sadie, the bad guy would not. Food would be secreted in Sadie's enclosure while she was watching. Then one or the other trainer would enter. If it was the good guy, Sadie would engage in a conversation (hand signals, etc.) and help the trainer find the food, but she would do her best to withhold information and even to mislead the bad guy.

Now it is possible that Sadie simply figured out via conditioning what the best way was, given the situations presented, to get her reward, but the experiments strongly suggest a degree of premeditation and intentionality. In other words, Sadie was thinking about it.

In one way of regarding such things, deceit and cheating may have played a significant role in the origins and development of intellect. That is because deceit and cheating are the reverse of reciprocal altruism, which is practiced among many animals besides humans – most notably, perhaps, among our primate cousins, though birds have been found to practice it as well. In the Gombe Reserve, for example, scientists often spot a male baboon enlisting the aid of another male to help attack a third male, usually when the third one is involved with an estrous female. Typically in such situations the first baboon runs off with the female while the enlistee and the cuckold finish the fight. In the words of Colin Beer of Rutgers, the "solicited male gets the blows while his friend gets the girl." Importantly, observers have found that more often than not the collusive male later asks for the same favor and it is granted. Long-term partnerships form from such cooperation.

For such a situation to arise – and work well enough to continue – several factors must be present. First, the society in question has to be small enough so that all the members can recognize each other. (You wouldn't expect a pair of anonymous seagull con artists to team up.) Second, the group has to be stable enough over time to provide opportunities for the repetitive getting and giving of assistance. And the members of the group have to be smart enough to keep score.

Even so, given the notion that it is to a male's advantage to sow his genes as far and wide as possible, there could be a payoff for a cheater. A blatant cheater who accepted help but never proffered it in return would probably not get away with it for very long before being ostracized, but this still leaves considerable inducement for ever more clever attempts to cheat (like the hamadryas pair consorting behind the rock). And this in turn would force the altruists in the society to become ever more clever in spotting deceitful behavior.

Some scientists have suggested that it was precisely this kind of "arms race" between two strategies – cheating and altruism – that ultimately escalated into the highest form of intelligence we know: ours. (A humbling thought.) But certainly, the kind of altruism observed in the Gombe baboons cannot be understood as anything but intentional. One animal must persuade another that it wants help and that it will return the favor. That sounds like thinking.

This area of science is a perilous thicket, replete with problems of definition as well as of experimental design and interpretation. The squabbles, if polite, are largely nonstop. But today a growing number of scientists are beginning to peer through that species-specific membrane that separates us, so completely it seems, from the rest of animal life and, perhaps, mind. As different as we are from other animals, we share an enormous array of physiological, biochemical, and behavioral similarities. The submicroscopic sites throughout our organs at which we receive the molecular information generated from glands including the Big Gland, our brain, and thus learn what is expected of them at any moment, are made up of the same series of amino acids as the equivalent receptors of a snail. As Carolyn Ristau has said: "We and most existent animal life have nervous systems that are remarkably similar, and most neurons are connected by synapses that also seem quite similar. If we wish to assume other species are not conscious, what is it that is so distinctly different about our nervous system that precludes consciousness in other species?"

And if it turns out that animals are self-aware, are conscious, are thinking some of the time in a manner akin to us, what shall we do?

We might have to rid ourselves of the last vestiges of the idea of that "great chain of being" that so securely places humanity alone and smug on the top. We might be impelled to regard ourselves as one among many expressions of life – a different idea than being high man on the totem pole. Already, most people get upset by the thought of harming such evidently sentient creatures as whales and porpoises, apes and, of course, pets – even for scientific purposes. But how far down the great chain should we go? Where does thinking begin? With birds?

Griffin sees a kind of primitive thinking ability even in honeybees, which are capable of dealing with utterly new situations in ways that suggest a glimmer of cognition. By virtue of their famous "dance," scout bees convey to the rest of the hive not only that they have found a good source of nectar (or a suitable new nest cavity), but also in what direction it lies and how far away it is. Furthermore, one scout who has found a good nectar source can have its "mind" changed by a scout who's uncovered a superior source.

We may have to rethink our entire attitude about animals as merely reflexive automata. And somewhere along the chain of being, we may reach a point that will throw into confusion or obsolescence our tendency to generalize, to think in abstractions. Today, even scientists actively engaged in trying to save endangered species are doing just that: saving what is, at least from an individual animal's point of view, an abstraction.

But if some animals think, then it is likely that individual animals within a species don't always think alike. We may have to begin considering animals – at least many kinds of animals – as individuals with individual consciousnesses and, it follows, individual rights. In fact, if Griffin et al. are right, a lot of people including many scientists will find themselves in a difficult moral pickle.

Morality does not arise from science, which is mere knowledge; it comes most gracefully from religion. But Western religion says little about this matter except that animals are without souls. It is probably too late for most of us to return to animism, but even those tribal societies that attributed not just cognition but souls to animals had well-worked-out ways of dealing with the morality of their use. And use them they did, as humans (who are omnivores) must as a matter of biological law. Our society has no moral principles on this matter on which reasonable people agree. That is to say, outside of true-believers and fanatics of various stripes, we are confused about our place in nature. And if we are confused about *that*, what else is certain? One thing, perhaps: inquiries into such areas of ignorance as the possibility that seagulls and baboons can practice deceit are more important than we might heretofore have thought.

Hay's Terns

TERNS HAVE ALWAYS made me feel good. This sensation began when I first took notice of an undifferentiated array of mostly white birds playing over the surf while I played in the sand out of the surf's reach. Those were the days not so much of innocence as of perfection, or as close as one gets, given the unavoidable fact that we are part of an unfinished universe.

Later I realized that there were distinctions to be made between terns and gulls and the other birds, and later again I realized you could even make distinctions among terns. All of these distinctions merely added to the tern-mediated feeling of well-being I experience when I see them or have them in my mind's eye. But it took a man named John Hay to give me the sense that these maritime nomads are connected to, or may even be part of, my soul.

John Hay is a quintessential prober of those opaque windows that seem to separate us from the rest of nature. This is not to say that he is a scientist, designing stimulus/response tests to learn about the mental world of the dolphin or otherwise reducing life to measurable and inert components, as so many (though not all) scientists do. John Hay is mostly in favor of science but that simply isn't what he does. He is a nature writer. He observes and yearns his way to understanding.

For a time he was a newspaperman and in 1950 found himself in Los Alamos which, he concluded, "was the ultimate in the abstract idea of practicality, an end product made almost without human contact." He decided that "a secret violence without any obligations to life could not even give any importance to death." So in due course, after newspapering here and there, he wound up on Cape Cod, haunting the intertidal zone and seeing to the sea and the weather. He retained his classy native New Hampshire accent and his flinty skepticism about humanity's grandeur, knowing that something of importance lived out there. After a time, he wrote a book about alewives. These are migratory fish, and fish are about the most distant from us, the most opaque, of all vertebrates. But John Hay got into alewives and found himself embroiled in planetary rhythms.

Most naturalists get embroiled in these rhythms and most people don't read nature books. There is an unfortunately small universe, nearly closed, of nature writers, nature book reviewers, and nature book readers. A fine choir. It should be expanded, because a lot of people die from diseases brought on by stress which can now be defined as a loss of adaptation to the natural rhythms of life. Maybe books about planetary rhythms should be more widely circulated. Pass them along; don't keep any nature books except field guides.

Anyway, after alewives, John Hay looked in on the lives of terns. Unable to migrate the thousands of miles terns do, he waited for them on the shore: "The season gradually delivers them and they start to grow again. In and out of the ocean waters and the long shores winding down to the southern continent, in and out of snow squalls, sun spearing through mountainous clouds, water spouts, and rain, lowlying mists, thick fog, and that brilliant light free again to ripen the waters, they drift in crying."

From the ground he watched the courtship flight of the roseate terns: "At times they skate through the sky as if shot from a sling, and at others they sail and float as buoyantly as a kite on a high wind; or they knife quickly through the air like mackerel in undulant waters. They remind me of Blake's 'arrows of desire.' "

Compulsively I quote John Hay, here on the topic of tern sex, a chaotic business: "In a community of terns – males and females trying to relate, to set up housekeeping and produce offspring, all in a very short season – the process often looks quite frenzied. Yet perhaps they are only as persistent and compulsive in their ways as human beings acting on imperative inner demands throughout their own lives. Which is more unconscious than the other?"

Then the hunt.

"The arrow bird hovers over the water and makes a quick pitch in, coming up with a small silvery fish. It has the skill of all fishing people, and of any number of other lives that fly in, swim out, reach for their fulfillment, and die in a minute or a year, being, for all they know immortally bound. The sun-braided waters sway along the shore, and they carry a depth of response we can only sense."

Or perhaps we are losing the sense to respond.

Maybe our civilization, which is an affair evolved from acquired characteristics, will finally have so profound an effect that we will become biologically incapable of seeing terns. Who will tell us when we have stepped beyond that pale? After all, we can orbit the planet much faster than terns can.

For now, we can stand beside John Hay at night in "the oldest place on earth," the zone where sea meets land, the place where the rhythmicity of life almost certainly first took place and biological time – the only important kind of time – was invented. "On the fringe of these teeming worlds, hearing the cold currents of the tide run by and its waters trickling through the rockweed, lifted by the exalted cover of uncountable stars, I have felt an inclusion that I have never experienced anywhere else. If God is dead, or missing in action, this might be the place to recover him again."

Occasionally John Hay worries that as a classic, old-style naturalist, he may be a man who is out of his time. But usually at such moments something catches his eye – the first alewife of the season, perhaps – and he is suddenly too busy to fret. Such people are rare, possibly endangered. To me they are sacrosanct. They do not need us to honor them, only to learn to see a bit more clearly with the help of their eyes. No such singer of the sea can be a man out of his time.

The Razor's Edge

I DON'T LIKE TO BE away from home for long in May, since that is when the irises bloom. To my mind they are the most satisfying of flowers. The pale blue-green samurai-sword leaves provide needed texture to any garden. The buds, as they emerge above the leaves, appear to be wrapped in paper, like any proper gift. And then, when the flower itself emerges, it is clearly the design of an oriental artist of old, rendered on the finest of rice paper. Logic suggests that all irises must be Japanese but for the most part they aren't. There are delicate little ones that are Asian in origin, but irises were known in ancient Greece and Egypt; there is evidence that those people ate the iris tubers, a ridiculous waste.

Inland wonders notwithstanding, a short visit to the Atlantic beach in early May is in order. It's too cold to swim and there is none of the raging drama of the winter beach. But there aren't a whole lot of people there in May. A cold wind blows, the last reminder of winter we'll receive for many months. The sand swirls up and falls, the result of boulders that have gradually been ground down to an infinitude of fine grains. The sand is a reminder that we – mankind – live in an interval, the interval between the last ice age and the next. It was the ice ages that gave us most of the beaches, and also probably most of what we consider civilization.

Some say it was the cold from advancing and retreating ice sheets that led early humans to use their heads (then filling up with neural connections in an amplitude of cortex) and invent such things as clothes. It takes a little hardship, so conventional wisdom goes, to alert people to the need for change. If mankind – lacking curiosity or population pressure or whatever – had not moved out of the tropics long ago and into more straitened environs, we might all still be idling away our days in hammocks, winging the occasional bird or squirrel with a rock, and eating locally foraged health foods. Instead, impelled by the chill, our minds grew and with them our ambitions.

It was evidently around this time or a little earlier that the beaches of the world entered a period of growth. Just after the last ice age, in a period called the Holocene, a major worldwide phase of beach-building began as the climate, sea level, rainfall, and patterns of ocean currents all shifted. Erosion from glacier-ground lands brought rocky material out of the hills to be milled in rushing streams and rivers, winding up as sand that spread, down-drift, along the shores into beaches. For millions of years, beaches grew to what they are now, a gift of the ice ages.

People usually come to the beach to enjoy a parenthetical peace in the busy paragraph of the year, but beaches are among the most tension-ridden places in the world, if you think about it. They are margins, on the move, insecure. In mid-May the beach here, south of Delaware Bay, looks like Verdun with cast-off helmets lying all around: horseshoe crabs late to leave last night's orgy. It's a disturbing sight. A few early terns thrash the southbound breeze and a willet calls desperately. Four ruddy turnstones – tweedy Ivy Leaguers – politely poke the intertidal sand. The spring tide has been unkind to beach decor, producing precipitous berms and races, drop-offs, channels, all challenges in the present armed landing which seems difficult enough without this additional topographic treachery. But the horseshoe crabs have been doing this a long time. In their unimaginably long history, they have had to follow this particular shore – narrow or wide – eastward all the way from what is now Africa, once Pangea broke up and the continents began to drift apart.

The warriors that remain on the beach are all females. The smaller males, having hitched a ride ashore on the female's carapaces, did their year's work in a trice and quickly fled back to the sea. Many of the females remaining here are waiting patiently for the indignity of being tumbled back into the water by the waves – or for an even worse indignity. Many, lying upside down, are already dead, having up-ended too high above the spring tide's now receding reach. Armed landings on beaches have always taken a toll.

Certainly the horseshoe crabs appear well armed. Many beach-goers fear the lancelike tail, yet it is not, according to biologists, a weapon. It is a device the animal can use to right itself if it gets rolled. Judging from the scene here just south of the center of horseshoe crabdom, the tail is a device that needs a bit more evolutionary work, even though these trilobitic ladies trace their lineage some 350 million years back to the Paleozoic, before the continents got divorced.

As ever, the horseshoe crabs (called *Limulus*) have laid their eggs here – a tidy array of some eighty thousand green jelly-like eggs are deposited by each female a few inches under the moist sand. This is evidently safer than letting them go in the sea, what with eels and minnows and all lurking around predaciously. It also suggests that, formerly, *Limulus* or its forebears were land animals that took to the water, returning to the land annually for their most important chore (the reverse of, say, toads).

But life played a trick on the horseshoe crab. It went on to evolve reptiles, birds, and mammals. Soon now this beach and its green egg-deposits will be a fast-food way station. Timing is everything and there are a lot of clocks involved in this coastal franchise. Before long, millions of hungry shore birds will go through here on their way north from Peruvian beaches, Surinam mud flats, even the rocky coasts of

Patagonia, driven by their own internal biological clocks and their own subtle readings of the sun. The crabs, on the other hand, seem to respond more to the phases of the moon, water temperatures, and the cycle of the tides.

North of here, Delaware Bay is a major staging area for all kinds of shore birds – peeps, turnstones, dunlins, plovers, oyster catchers, avocets, sandpipers, and especially red knots. Millions of them. Many of these birds will as much as double their weight in a feeding frenzy made possible by *Limulus,* gaining the energy needed to fly another two to three thousand miles northward, arriving at their breeding areas just as the snow is melting on the tundra. If they arrive too late, their young hatchlings (who feed themselves) will miss the great hatches of insects in early July. But the crabs are never late.

It has been calculated that for a sanderling to double its weight along this shore in the two weeks it spends here, it must eat 135,000 *Limulus* eggs, or one every five seconds for fourteen hours a day. So fifty thousand sanderlings would consume some six billion eggs. It is pleasant to think that something with so ancient a lineage as *Limulus,* here compliments of the trilobites (never mind the less ancient lineage of dinosaurs that spawned birds), has played a role in avian survival.

Whatever horseshoe crab eggs are left after this kindness to shore birds have a mere two weeks to do their complex embryonic work – a series of moults within the egg's outer membrane – before the sun, earth, and moon line up and produce the little spring tide. With this nice precision timing, the larvae (which resemble trilobites almost exactly) will be promptly washed out to sea, many of them no doubt into the maws of predators.

All in all, it works. The horseshoe crab is just the same now as it was in the Triassic (dinosaur time): there has been no reason, evidently, for physiological or behavioral change. Happy as a clam, as they say. Each one, equipped with its own biological chronometer, metronomically imposing its own sense of order on the tumultuous changing environment of the sea and shore, emerging on cue from the muck way off on the continental shelf as spring comes, cruising along the bottom, picking off the occasional marine worm, tuned to the moon, tick, tock, doing its yeomanlike (mainly yeowomanlike, I mean) work on the beach every year for hundreds of millions of years: the archest of conservatives.

Time and environment have been kind. The horseshoe crab even survived the trick that produced shore birds. But of course humanity has not been so kind. People along the East Coast used to grind them up by the thousands for fertilizer (till cheaper alternatives came along) and chicken feed (till people complained that the *Limulus*-fed chickens tasted lousy).

Scientists, particularly at Wood's Hole, found their primitive eyes and nerve cells perfect for exploring the mysteries of vision and the functioning and dysfunctioning of nerve systems. Laboratory use was cost-effective; from a relatively few horseshoe crabs, we have learned much about our own visual system and have obtained important insights into the likes of Lou Gehrig's disease.

But then science found out about *Limulus* blood. It turns out, to be brief, that as part of its immune system, *Limulus*'s blood contains large amoeba-like cells which race to the scene of a bacterial infection and devour the intruders. But in the presence of certain kinds of so-called gram-negative bacteria, the system backfires in such a way as to kill the horseshoe crab. At any rate, it soon became clear that *Limulus* blood acted the way rabbit blood does, only quicker. It was not long before a treated version of *Limulus* blood, called a lysate, became the substance of choice in hospitals to test for certain toxins in humans. For example, in the case of spinal meningitis, the rabbit test takes a perilous forty-eight hours; the *Limulus* derivative takes only an hour.

So today commercial companies collect gravid horseshoe crabs by the thousands, bleed them, and according to FDA regulations, throw them back, live, into the sea within seventy-two hours. At one typical plant, which bleeds some five hundred females a day for seven months a year, half died before being returned to the sea, with many more

dying shortly thereafter. The FDA is trying to tighten up the regulations, but the voracious demand from the pharmaceutical companies
continues and, for unassailable reasons, will continue to do so for the
foreseeable future.

The states of New Jersey and Delaware have declared one strip of
beach a horseshoe crab sanctuary, but not so much for the sake of
Limulus. Rather, protection is afforded them because their eggs feed
the migratory shore birds, something we can all celebrate. This move
by the two states is terribly important, but I suspect that someone with
an abacus or a computer could describe exactly how much more beach
front needs to be given over to horseshoe crabs if we are to permit these
millions of shore birds to continue to exist. The places where *Limulus*
congregate may be considered in the same manner as an oasis on a
traditional route through a desert. The flyway that includes Delaware
Bay starts far to the south and ends far to the north. The loss of one
oasis along the way could spell the end of the shore birds (which are so
easily taken for granted, given their sheer numbers). Only two migrat-
ing shore birds known to this continent are considered endangered –
the piping plover and the Eskimo curlew – but all the shore birds that
flow northward up the planet each spring, then southward in the fall,
live a fragile life indeed, owing their existence now to the ability we can
muster locally to provide sufficient room for the horseshoe crabs to go
about their far more ancient rites.

The horseshoe crabs have survived many great intervals such as the
one we and the red knots live in. It is possible they will survive into the
next, given their simple persistence. That we are on the cusp of a new
interval may be suggested by the fact that recently the beaches have
begun to recede. This can be seen along the Atlantic beach as clearly as
anywhere else. The lighthouse at Cape Hatteras used to rise above a
beach that stretched out hundreds of yards before it felt the lap of the
waves. Now it is perched parlously close to the sea. Storms, people say.
A single hurricane in the 1920s in Florida accounted for fifty percent of
the local beach loss in this century.

One summer, on a visit to the Outer Banks of North Carolina, I was stunned to find an enormous pipe some five feet in diameter running up and down the beach as far as the eye could see. A severe winter storm, I was told, had made an unacceptable incursion, carrying off too much of the beach upon which local innkeepers made their livings and to which people like me came to forget about making a living. The Corps of Engineers was piping a slurry of sand and seawater north to replenish the beach.

Winter storms take much of the blame for beach loss, and with reason. But a process called littoral drift is always – summer and winter – moving the beach. For example, waves and currents have a geophysical tendency to smooth things out, shaving away at promontories. Confronted by an obstacle like a promontory, a passing current tends to speed up, just like water in a stream. So, given time, such places become straight-edged, evened out, like the South Beach on Martha's Vineyard. And given more time, they disappear. It is estimated that Cape Cod and Martha's Vineyard, not to mention Nantucket, will be no more by the year 4000.

Locals will tell you, and common sense suggests, that what the sea taketh away, it replaceth down-drift. Cape Cod is thus seen to be very slowly "rolling over," just as many barrier islands move, change shape and position. People who own beachfront property, though aware of these grand natural redesignings, are likely to be unphilosophical about them and have, from time to time, resorted to constructing groins and seawalls and other unsightly Canutian solutions, even asking government agencies to reverse the littoral drift by main force and pipelines. Such ploys don't work. The pipeline no longer graces the Outer Banks.

And there *is* nothing like a storm to hasten the redesign of beaches. A nice, playful summer wave – about, say, ten feet tall and a hundred feet long – exerts a pressure of 1,600 pounds against every square foot of shoreline it strikes. A typical winter storm wave exerts four times that, ample to erode a seawall in due course, much less a beach of sand.

And no storm is more devastating to a beach and its inhabitants than a hurricane – actually an autumnal affair.

Scientists have become more knowledgeable about these awesome spiral galaxies of wind and cloud that take form in the western Atlantic and the Caribbean to sweep around the sea and, often, barge inland. In an average year, five hurricanes arise from quantities of smaller tropical cyclonic storms, which are all driven by titanic heat engines. The heat is liberated from the condensation of moisture at a nearly unimaginable rate. In one day a hurricane can produce heat energy equivalent to some two trillion kilowatt-hours – about a year's electrical output in the United States.

The transfer of energy in hurricanes from heat to kinetic energy (wind) is inefficient – about three percent – but this is sufficient to generate winds of up to two hundred miles per hour. Such winds and the waves they produce are devastating in themselves, but what is worse is what is called the storm surge. The winds and low pressure around a hurricane's eye can raise the level of the ocean some two feet in an area fifty miles across. As the surge nears shore, bottom conditions can cause the dome of water to rise as much as twenty feet above sea level. Add that to wind-waves and a high tide and the name is catastrophe – the most awesome and destructive of all natural catastrophes.

But hurricanes are getting more predictable. Meteorologists can now trace these storms to such subtle matters as perturbations in a thin current of air that flows westward between the Sahara and the cooler lands south. Few human beach dwellers are now likely to be taken by surprise by hurricanes, but these storms will always carry off beaches.

There are winter storms, however, that in the aggregate can cause as much trouble as hurricanes. These are called – a bit quaintly – "bombs" by meteorologists, who are yet to understand them. Commonly seen off the coast of the Carolinas, they arise very quickly from areas of low atmospheric pressure. In a day or less, an innocuous storm system covering a fairly large area can develop unpredictably into a more concentrated cyclonic fury.

A few years ago, some two hundred scientists and technicians, armed with radar equipment, aircraft, and other monitoring devices, spent two months trying to get to the bottom of these storms in a project called the Genesis of Atlantic Lows Experiment (GALE). Get it? It seems that there is a recipe of meteorological ingredients needed for a bomb to arise.

The Appalachians, for example, have to be damming up cold air so that warm oceanic air floating in over the cold air provides a temperature gradient sufficient to energize the system. Also the Gulf Stream's surface temperature must be far greater (about fifteen degrees Fahrenheit) than the surrounding air, so that the lower atmosphere becomes destabilized by the rising warmth. An east-flowing jet of air called the warm conveyor belt then sends streaks of moisture and energy into the storm at specific, localized places. Higher up, local differences in the speed of the jet stream cause vertical motions of air, and its descent (called the tropopause) starts things rotating down below. At the same time bands of rain over the Gulf Stream may energize the system, as does the surprisingly large amount of lightning the scientists found over the Gulf Stream.

It takes many culprits to cause such a natural conspiracy and scientists are still far from understanding just how they interact. Meanwhile these ocean-bred storms (with warmer cores, they are more energetic than land-bred storms with cold cores) will continue to flay the shoreline unpredictably.

In fact, when it comes to beaches, the odds are like those quoted by Damon Runyon concerning just about everything: six-to-five against. A recent study shows that virtually everywhere in the world, even in remote places where no dams prevent riverine silt and sand from replenishing the shoreline, there is now an overwhelming domination of erosion over growth. The sea takes but it doesn't necessarily replace. Nobody knows why beach growth has been reversed globally. The reasons could vary locally or be part of some yet-to-be understood overall dance of the ocean, climate, and land.

Meanwhile I sit here on the beach among a lot of horseshoe crab ladies, each in personal trouble. I think about the thousands of shore birds who depend on these fecund creatures and the possibility that mankind could easily limit them and thus limit the birds to the point where the grand migration of airborne nomads will one day simply peter out. We are a phylumocentric group: anything with a backbone gets one degree or another of our sympathy or at least respect. There are not many invertebrates on the endangered species lists. If you are without a spinal column, you are mere cannon fodder in someone else's war.

With nothing better to do and feeling oddly guilty, my wife and I spend an hour throwing stranded horseshoe crabs back into the ocean.

Good luck, ma'am. Good luck.

Aphrodisia and Zebra Finches

IN A THREE-WINDOW BAY in a front room of my house is a flight cage five feet high, six feet wide, and two feet deep. For most of the day, light streams in and seven finches flutter in and out of the shade of large ferns. They seem to enjoy themselves well enough. Three are survivors of the great empire of finches that once lived among us. Indeed, they are long since widowed, all of them gentle and even a bit melancholy in their survivorship. One, the violet-eared waxbill, is of extraordinary color – dark purply-blue and a rich brown like dark suede, with a bright red eye and bill. It is he who sings the vespers, a long liquid series of notes of wonderful subtlety and variety. These days, being ancient for a finch, he cozies up with a widower orange-cheeked waxbill, like two old people in a retirement home who would have had nothing to do with each other in earlier, reproductive days but now, under the circumstances, what the hell . . . company is more important than the silly distinctions of youth. The other singleton is a lavender waxbill – not lavender but pearly grey and maroon – which retains its species-specific curiosity with age, still the first to check out anything new. There is also a new pair of spice finches, quiet burghers with little white spots on their brown plumage; they remain respectful in the midst of these classy oldsters, to the point that they haven't yet filled the flight cage with the annoying squalling of infant spice finches. And then there are the zebra finches.

Zebra finches are good to start with if you want finches and you want success – that is, success measured in reproductive capacity. These are sporty little birds, native to Australia, mostly grey with black-and-white striped tails, orange bills and, among males, orange legs, and orange circles on their cheeks. They are loud and a bit pushy and you have to be an utterly incompetent finch-keeper if your zebra finches do not reproduce. I can imagine nothing by way of obstruction or interference that will keep these little birds from producing brood after brood – three or four eggs at a time – as regularly as fleas. Not long ago, as what he may have believed was an act of generosity, a son-in-law gave us two zebra finches and within about the time it takes to do the Sunday crossword puzzle there were six of them in the cage with four more eggs sitting ominously in the nest. Alarmed, we raced off to a lady named Ginger who ran the local pet store and she agreed, with an ashen countenance and polite smile, to take the young off our hands. Next, we dragooned the man who delivers for Federal Express, persuading him that *his* young brood of children needed nothing less than the next finches to hatch to foster in them a lasting reverence for life. He accepted this as true and we played a trick: we gave him all the zebras but for two males. So now we have two bachelors and, without their sole interest in view, they have calmed down a bit.

And thus did I give up the possibility of getting my name in the scientific literature again. (Once, I made idle note in print that woolly bear caterpillars all seem determined to cross roads and that they all somehow knew how to cross the road by the most direct route. You never see a woolly bear going across a road on the diagonal: always straight across, even choosing the shortest route when they cross at a curve. Later I found myself quoted in an article in the august journal *The American Naturalist*, which showed, as I recall it, that woolly bear caterpillars have a refined sense of infrared which somehow leads to this efficiency.) But if I had looked into zebra finch behavior carefully, and built about fifteen more flight cages for them to fill up, I could possibly have added data to a particularly angry debate that broke out among scientists a while back. Scientists do get angry at each other, as cool as the enterprise is supposed to seem to the public, and you can tell, even in the articles that occur in professional journals, when they've got their hackles up. In the instance I am referring to, the angst and anger was about zebra finches, as silly as that may seem.

The chief issue was the question of how nature regulates the numbers of each sex so as to create a proper balance. Generally speaking, equal numbers of each would seem best . . . except in hard times. Then, it would seem effective to produce members of the sex that is least costly to raise, or the most useful to have around.

We civilized humans tend to leave such matters to the luck of the draw even though we can now foretell the sex of a baby, thanks to biomedical techniques. Soon we may be able to intervene routinely and determine in advance the gender of our offspring. And in a society like ours, where roles are changing and where the effects of advertising and consumerism seem more powerful than formal education, there is no telling what havoc might result. We are bent on being free of the restraints of nature and whatever wisdom is embodied in nature after all these eons, and if a generation or so of gender-options swing society drastically in one direction or another, the nature of human society and life could be almost unrecognizable. We run the process of evolution these days, or soon will, without understanding it. So it's probably a good idea that a few scientists are rather frantically trying to understand how nature works before we hold our nose and jump into the gene pool feet first with our eyes essentially closed.

There are extreme ways of handling this matter. In the dreadful conditions in which the Netsilik Eskimos carried out their traditional culture, it was of paramount importance to have plenty of males around to do the hunting, so about one-third of all female babies born were simply dispatched. Icy-minded ethnographers of today have taken this old data on the Netsilik and run it through a computer. The first printout said that, at that rate of female infanticide, the Netsilik had completely died out as a culture long before the first ethnographers arrived, which of course they hadn't. Once the modern ethnographers recalled that breast-feeding a baby for a couple of years serves as a contraceptive measure and that, without their newborn female infants, Netsilik mothers had more babies, the computers confirmed a steady-state population for traditional Netsilik. This seems an awfully cold-blooded way to handle things, but nature tends to be cold-blooded in the long run – all the more reason to see how nature works before we arrogate to ourselves and our momentary whims and myths the design of everything we hold dear.

It has been found, for example, that in hard times wood rat mothers discriminate against their sons. The males get less food and thus they grow less, reproduce less, and die younger. But there are a lot of wood rats, through thick and thin. It turns out that small, slightly starved female wood rats can produce the same size litters as better fed ones, while slightly starved males are simply good for nothing. How do wood rats "know" this? Earnest people were fretting about such things and designing experiments to answer them when Nancy Burley of the University of Illinois noticed something strange about her zebra finches and, in 1981, threw a sinkerball into the entire discussion.

It's pretty hard to keep track of a large group of zebra finches so, to help distinguish one from the other, Burley took the well-established path of banding their little legs with different colored plastic bands. She soon noticed that female zebra finches spent a lot more time "approaching" (i.e., vamping) males that had red or orange bands than they did unbanded males. Similarly, they tended to avoid males with blue or green bands. Equally, males seemed to prefer black-banded females and treated as wallflowers those with blue bands. Burley figured that the bands could hype what was already attractive about the bird: males would be seen as even brighter orange swingers; females would be given a further edge in sultriness, as with a naughty piece of lingerie from Victoria's Secret. And if attractiveness has something to do with the ultimate balance of the sexes, Burley further hypothesized, then a wimpy green-banded male who somehow managed to garner a black-banded honey would tend to produce few males and many females. And vice-versa. Burley's published results seem to bear this out. But, perhaps innocently, she walked into an ornithological buzz saw in the form of three zoologists at the University of Wisconsin led by Klaus Immelmann who was billed in those days as "something of an expert on mate choice and breeding in the zebra finch." (I was astonished at the time to find that there was someone who had taken the time to develop such expertise: certainly zebra finches don't need much counseling.) In any event, Immelmann et al. roundly attacked Burley's results, citing fourteen experimental sins including overcrowding, not finding out if renesting birds retained the same mates, bad statistical analysis, and the presence of a lesbian pair which raised some young, an indiscretion that cast a pall of "behavioral pathology" over the entire sixty-adult experiment.

Most people I know, if so thoroughly devastated in print, would pack up their finches and take them to Ginger, and go into another line of work. But Burley persisted. She tried again, this time using fewer birds and two species: zebra finches and double-bar finches, both from the same Australian genus. The double-bars are less colorful than zebras; both sexes look the same; and their beaks and legs are bluish-grey.

Burley gave males and females of both species a choice between three target birds – with red bands, blue bands, and no bands. The zebras went mostly for those with red bands; the double-bars opted strongly for blue bands. Burley was satisfied that her theory is correct: finches fall for other finches who have "exaggerated identity marks," those in short who have been gaudily color-enhanced. Such a built-in preference for extremes in plumage might be the little evolutionary engine that led all these finches to separate into distinctively feathered species in Australia, Burley opines, and there the matter rests.

While these findings may provide some additional insights for the cosmetics industry, I am afraid they do not – in spite of the intensity of the debate they sparked – provide us with much wisdom about how to regulate the proportion of the sexes. I would happily volunteer my two male zebra finches to any further research along these lines but, I confess, they have by now become quite friendly and, in any experiment they took part in, some sourpuss would probably cite them as an example of behavioral pathology.

Redbird

IT IS ONE OF THOSE DAYS when a snowfall has settled down to sulk on the landscape and melt. The sky is a uniformly opaque grey, the hedgerow a murky black-brown. The day is short. What light we are permitted is diffuse and without definition: the crisp delights of winter have temporarily turned into old celery. A great dampness. There are people who become frightfully depressed at such times and some of them regain their composure only, medical science seems to think, if they spend part of the day under Gro-lite lamps, the sort used for house plants. For others, there are less cumbersome solutions.

A cardinal appears, a little packet of tropiclike joy on a wet black twig in a disheveled bush outside, and suddenly there is a small, significant change in the local universe. Color returns for an instant – a magical, timeless instant – focused by the bird's brilliant feathers. For just a moment in the damp, grey emulsion of winter, there is a miniburst of elation, and hope hinges on this bird.

Hope? Hope for what, asks the rationalist?

This is not an easy time for nature writers, the kind of people who have traditionally sought to share the comfort they find in the change of the season, the veins of a leaf, or the apparition of a common bird in the still-life of a winter afternoon. We are told that there is little meaning in such things, never mind one's emotional life – little left that is translatable into a philosophy for making one's way through the days and the nights. This is because they let physicists loose in this realm. Physicists lately presume to be the accounting department of nature, woebegone anchors attached to otherwise free-sailing yachts.

Today, to know nature is to know that it consists mostly of empty spaces inhabited by flashing instants of subatomic energy packets appearing here, then there, evidently without cause. This sounds absurd, of course, but believe me: this is the world according to physics. Nature as you and I perceive it may not even exist in the sense of being real, except that it will respond to a physicist with an answer determined only by the question he asks. Worse, to seek ethical principles from nature is to anthropomorphize it and this is a sin. That there can be sins in a natural world devoid of meaning may seem paradoxical, but not if you are a physicist and have laid claim to the rules of the game. Such is the legacy of the physicists' new world view, quantum mechanics: we populate a dream and no one knows whose dream it is.

Theologians and philosophers, even some physicists, have set out to find god, or at least to redefine god, in this rarefied quantum broth, and what may be emerging is at least a sign of an orderly geometric urge that lies behind the Big-Bang origins of our universe. All paradox – and very thin soup indeed. The cardinal outside is at best a temporary fancy in one enormous thought. Same for the rest of us. Under the circumstances, it may make little sense to take up the cause of the cardinal, recently humiliated in print, but one does so anyway, in the hope that a bit of chivalry may lead somewhere useful in the chimerical plane where we obstinately carry on what we are pleased to call our existence.

Some time ago, a writer in *Smithsonian* saw fit to giggle at the expense of six state legislatures which, at various times in the past, unimaginatively chose the cardinal as their state bird. To be sure, the writer doffed his hat at the cardinal's excellent character, noting that the male is an especially adept parent. But he complained that no great raptors, no delightful warblers, not even that burgherlike choice of Ben Franklin's, the wild turkey, had made it onto the roster of state birds.

The male cardinal *is* a good parent, almost exclusively raising the young in spring, an exemplary provider, an ardent and patient teacher of fledglings. And so he must be: his equally exemplary mate is too busy hatching a second clutch of eggs. This activity suggests more virtue, as we see such things, than the sleazy scams of the cowbird, but I am told it can serve us ill in the long run to project our own, often temporary mores upon the actions of creatures we don't really understand all that well.

For example, in a book published in this century, there is the following paean to the virtues of the cardinal: "All through the Southern plantation country, this is the bird that typifies everything that is elegant and chivalric not only to the colored cotton pickers and plantation laborers, but to the country gentlemen."

Well.

Perhaps the scientists of today are right to perceive the cardinal merely as an interesting abstraction called a species, one of many such abstractions, driven by its own range of hormones and their response to light, all this mediated in the pineal gland, a kind of chemical machine that one could, if one wished, ultimately explain by reference to the nature of electrical potentials and the dance of subatomic energy packets. They, the biochemists, avoid a lot of grief by thinking in such a manner. Individual cardinals are, in such a way of thinking, dispensable: they are all merely role-players following a script written by a particular brand of selfish gene, window dressing for a self-replicating molecule.

What then am I to make of the male cardinal who spent an entire year attacking my kitchen window from a nearby bush? I would wake in the morning, hearing the insistent clatter as it hit the window, over and over, day in and day out, ignoring so far as I could see any parental or other duty, ceasing only when the sun went down.

A research ornithologist – my friend Gene Morton, in fact – suggested that the bird was attacking his own image in the window glass, but I looked at the window from the bird's angle and there was no image. Gene suggested that I place a mirror facing out of the window to see if the bird would attack it. It didn't. It's behavior was pointless and obviously counterproductive – an aberration assuring that whatever motivated this cardinal would not later turn up in the gene pool, evolution taking care of business, ridding the future of an automaton that had somehow become wrongly wired.

Even in the face of science's inability to explain this bird's behavior, it was patently silly for me to think of the aberrant tapping on the window as some sort of a sign, to take it personally as if some pattern in my own behavior was being cosmically frowned upon. Who needs avian reminders of that anyway? No omen here, just a neuronal screw-up, unfortunate for the bird but no reflection on human affairs.

Nevertheless, somewhere between a chemical mix-up leading to maniacal behavior by one cardinal and the magical apparition of another cardinal in a colorless snowscape, with my attendant dose of elation, there was something more than a valueless abstraction. There was something very real. It had to do with the fact that the bird is red.

The tanager is red, too, but it usually skulks in the woods while the cardinal moves in with us all year and stays red all year as well. Nothing about cardinals could be more important than their color, and this is probably why six state legislatures have adopted it. Red sells, say merchandising experts. Everything about the cardinal, it became clear, hinges on its very redness.

In fact, the Latin roots of the word *cardinal* mean hinge, and those exalted members of the early church were named for the crucial role they played in keeping ecclesiastic matters organized and functioning. And in those days when symbolic meanings had a more present reality than nowadays, red meant a host of things but none more present and powerful than the blood of the Savior, which is to say hope against the ineffable odds of the flesh. So, in some such manner, the cardinals of the European church came to wear red and it is no surprise at all how our bird came by its name.

In more recent history, red is also the symbol of anarchy and certain revolutions that did not turn out all that well – by our standards – and it is probably best here to take the line of the scientists and dismiss all those symbolic meanings and religious connotations as alien – certainly alien to the bird. And it is also probably best to stare scientific evidence right smack in the face if one is determined to find virtue or hope in the likes of a common red bird.

The cardinal is red because its feathers contain little packets of pigments – carotenes and others – that reflect the red wavelengths of light and absorb all the other wavelengths. Thus we see it as red. And red, science tells us, is but one component of visible light which itself is seen as white, and light is part of the larger electromagnetic spectrum which includes such esoterica as gamma rays and X rays, all having different properties in part because they have different wavelengths. The wavelength of red falls at about 620 nanometers on the scale and energy that oscillates at that precise rate produces a certain characteristic activity on the part of optic nerves, which in turn produces the sensation of red somewhere in the brain. That is about all that science has to say, in essence, about the red of the cardinal. More thin soup.

Indeed, the physics and chemistry of red are pretty well worked out up to the point of our having, in our brains, the sensation of red. It doesn't make sense to wonder if my wife sees the same red when she looks at the cardinal as I do. My neuronal system is operating on the same wavelength as hers and that is simply all that can be known. In fact, just what the *sensation* of red is lies beyond science, and herein lies hope. The language of science – which is fundamentally numerical – has no color. Numbers are colorless. Wavelengths are themselves colorless, as are photons. Chemical and physical reactions are colorless. There is no way that science can explain precisely what we know in our minds to be red.

Such anomalies as this have led some philosophers and even some physicists to suppose that there may be more to the mind than a material collection of neural activity, no matter how exquisitely complex it all might be as wiring or biochemical communication. It could be, they suggest, that mind (with its indescribable sense of red) exists beyond or somehow outside matter. Here again we may have what can be thought of as some hope against the ineffable odds of the flesh, a legitimization, at least, of the human sense of elation at the sight of beauty, quantum soup be damned.

The mind-matter question will plague thinkers for a long time. It may never be resolved. But it is enough to think that the answer to this conundrum could hinge on our ability to respond to something as commonplace as the cardinal, the little red burst in January's grey.

Marginal Stability

THE SCIENTISTS SEEM to have it all doped out now. Snow, I mean. The meteorologists, who seem to get more and more time on the newscasts, will give us a day or two of notice, often with considerable accuracy.

For example, you're driving up to a friend's place in the mountains that rise above Rockfish Valley in Nelson County, Virginia. It has been raining all day and the side valleys are filled with fog, bespeaking temperatures too high for snow. Yet the voice on the radio says it will snow by midnight. You arrive at the mountain aerie just before dark but there is nothing to see but rain-swept grey. It's as if you were suspended in a cloud.

The next morning it is clear and you look eastward over a phantasmagoria of shapes, the jumble of wooded, oddly misshapen foothills that lead up to where you stand. The foothills look like they have crewcuts. For it did snow lightly during the night, the way the man said, and the snow differentiates the ground from the brown leafless trees, much the way you can see a man's scalp around the side of his head if he has a military haircut.

Closer to, you notice that every branch, every twig, is adorned with a quarter-inch of snow that miraculously clings to the wood despite a brisk wind. No miracle, in fact. Conditions last night while you slept simply changed fast enough from rain to freezing rain to sleet and then snow so that the thin upper layer of snow is essentially glued to the branches by ice.

When I was a boy, snow seemed altogether miraculous – in fact, just about everything did. For years, to wake up and find the world so totally transformed by snow was akin to coming downstairs Christmas morning to discover the work of Santa Claus. Later, when I was old enough to take for granted that winter brought snowfalls, I found stunning the information that no snowflake, of the trillions that would fall in my yard, was exactly the same shape as any other. I tried to devise ways with a toy-store microscope to see this but, being untutored, I found no way to keep snowflakes intact until they were within range of my lens.

This ineptitude persisted in life: I have never "done" science. But I admire it for the most part and observe it with the awe of a mere mortal watching Fred Astaire.

Science has now explained the extraordinary variability of snowflakes. Because of the way molecules are arranged in water, water tends to grow hexagonal crystals when it freezes. For snow, it takes a particle of dust in the atmosphere to get the whole thing going. A tiny disk of ice forms around the mote, giving off a minuscule bit of heat as it does so. From then on, it's a matter of what physicists call marginal stability. If the ice were stable, it wouldn't grow. If it were altogether unstable, it wouldn't grow either. It grows best when it is, or part of it is, at marginal stability – a matter dictated by a number of things, mainly temperature and humidity.

As the little bit of ice begins to grow, it creates an initial instability by its tendency to crystallize in a flat, sixfold pattern. You get six little bulges, and each little bulge gives off a bit of latent heat which collects in between the bulges, restraining growth there, while the bulges continue to grow. As the emerging snowflake falls, it encounters changes in temperature and humidity – small changes but enough to affect the unstable parts of the flake. As the six branches grow, side structures will branch out from them and these in turn will branch with each new change in temperature and humidity. Because each branch encounters roughly the same conditions at the same time, they all tend to look alike, accounting for the baroque symmetry of snowflakes. But since each flake encounters ever-so-slightly different microconditions in its descent, no flake will look like any other, no matter how many fall.

Thus, coolly, does the scientist explain away the magic of snow. Now I know that most scientists have, and retain, an awe about the world in spite of their objective, unemotional explanations of its workings. But having explained snowflakes to their satisfaction, they are likely to move on to another subject, being a restless, curious lot. I prefer to return to common things, regardless of the state of our knowledge of them.

In the mountain aerie, another day brings another snow, fine snow, the kind that country wisdom suggests will go on a while and accumulate. You walk across meadows and down roads, the snow so fine or the temperature so low that nothing accumulates on your eyeglasses. But it does accumulate on the trees. The ends of branches, filigrees of twigs, are reversed now, pure white against lesser whites, greys, of more distant trees, off to an opaque place where all sense of definition is lost. Colorless, a cloud. Each tree trunk bears a vertical stripe of white on its windward side. On the edge of the stripes, snow defines the patterns of bark. The tree trunks now look like line drawings, a coloring-book forest waiting for someone with a crayon or two. An illusion, waiting to become real.

A tropical bird sound. You almost expect a feral macaw, bright blue and gold, to emerge into this black-and-white world, but a raven, black and ghostly, flies over, turning grey, then lost in the totally diffracted light – no highlights anywhere, no shadows, perfect light? Just the endlessly complex line drawing of the woods, the inexactness of distance, the quiet. It's as if you are walking in a glass-plate negative world.

Inside out. A world suddenly brought into focus by the passage of a lone bird.

Time, of course, that fundamental coefficient of the world, is lost in a place like this one as it fills up with snow. You can walk here in any century you choose.

Valentines

PEOPLE ARE INCLINED to knock the month of February. If it is the shortest month of the year, why does it seem so endlessly and disquietingly long? Though sorely tempted each year to follow suit, I make a Panglossian effort to find the best in everything, even the grey, damp, and cold times of February.

This month does, after all, bring us Valentine's Day, a cheerful event, more properly called St. Valentine's Day. (It also brings us George Washington's birthday, an event celebrated in shopping malls with considerable historic fanfare and with the statesmanlike appeals of commerce.)

Now Valentine, it seems, was a man who felt compelled to intercede on behalf of some early Christians. As is so often the case when one seeks to aid people, he became converted altogether to their cause and in due course became a priest in the Church. For this error in judgment, he was thrown in jail, that being the habit of the Romans who invented the basis of the laws by which we still live and who also loved jails, and Valentine soon discovered that his jailer's daughter was blind.

Valentine proceeded to restore the girl's sight. It is not said how this was done, nor is it important to know how he did it or whether he did it at all. What is important is that he went down in history as having done it, and that the Romans believed he had done it. Judging this quite marvelous act altogether subversive to their iron rule, they saw to it that on February 14, in the year 269, poor old Valentine was clubbed to death. For this martyrdom, he was subsequently proclaimed a saint. Or was he? It appears that a hundred or so years later there was another Valentine, also prominent in the affairs of the Church, and it is not altogether clear whether it was the earlier or later Valentine who was canonized. More February murk, unfortunately.

It may be wise to look at the pagan side of things, the old wisdom that preceded the rectitude of the early Church and the legalities of the Romans. In old England, February 14 was when people drew lots for lovers, a practice which no doubt helped that remote island kingdom to populate itself but a practice we must frown upon today as we would the clubbing of saints. And the one whose lot was drawn customarily offered the lot-holder a pair of gloves – the assumption being inevitable that the groundhog saw his shadow more often than not in those times and no one wants to be caressed by a new lover with cold hands. Nevertheless, I am afraid that here the pagans of Britain have let us down, as they rarely do.

The pagan custom of lot-drawing for love may have originated in an earlier belief that it was on February 14, no earlier and no later, that birds chose their mates.

Could this be true? Here would be a fact of nearly total relief for those facing February with a tendency to be grumpy. The evidence at hand is mixed, but definitely encouraging.

On a sunny day around mid-February, if there is one, anyone who ventures out into the yard with nothing much to do will hear a perceptible difference, a kind of gaiety in the air. The quiet wintry whisper song of the mockingbird seems to be gearing up toward its summer marvels. The incessant *queets* of the mob of house finches who have been swarming over the bird feeder are beginning to sound like music. And music among birds bespeaks, among other things, sex.

There are more avian ways of attracting mates – displays, dances, and the like – than there are avian species, but among perching birds a chief method is song. Not only does the song serve to attract females (it is mostly males that do the singing), but it advertises the male's hegemony over that particular nesting territory. And of the birds that are common moochers at my bird feeder, several are in full swing by mid-February. This month the flock of house finches could well break up, the females leaving singly, singing a warbling song, pursued avidly by a male. The Carolina chickadees and the titmice will nest this month, to lay eggs in March. Their songs clarify now. The mockingbird couple that hangs out year-round and nests in the wild rose in the hedgerow will produce eggs in March, as will the cardinal couple who now begin their remarkable repertoire of songs.

Others wait longer. The starlings won't produce eggs till early April, but in February I can hear them bustling around in the eaves of the house, making plans if not nests, and they are beginning to mimic the spring songs of other birds, as if to say, "I know what you sing. Get on with it." Nuthatches and grosbeaks are slow to get started and the female goldfinches remain altogether unimpressed with the opposite sex until the males turn yellow and the season has produced thistledown, with which they line their tiny nests.

Thus, however fitfully, is another old wives' tale shown to be partly true, as is so often the case, and the gloomy can rejoice with at least two cheers. And the birds' activities seem a bit more than the unemotional business of drawing lots.

Most of the birds that nest here in my yard seem to be monogamous, nesting together at least for several years in a row, but this I am told has little to do with romance. (And, alas, science tells us now that what seem monogamous affairs among birds are often rife with what are called "extra-pair copulations.") In any event, in a female's first year, she will drop in on the territories of several different singing males, eventually choosing one. Thereafter, she tends to become habituated to that nesting site and returns to it each year; if the same male is there, well and good. Or at least that's how ornithologists see it. But for those infected with the spirit of St. Valentine's Day, one does no harm either to oneself or to the birds by imagining that this new gaiety in the air in mid-February is a cheerful reaffirmation of comfortable relationships, just as a husband might send a wife of long standing a suggestive valentine.

Duck Weather

Day One: Chincoteague, Virginia.

Rain. Rain that would unnerve Noah. Even the dry places in the marshlands of the Atlantic Coast fill up with water – pine needle puddles, brand new canals reflecting in a rain-pocked chaos the unnaturally dark sky.

West of here, in the Piedmont and beyond, there is snow, freezing rain, sleet, all those tiresome products of the wintry midwest where, perhaps from living with a big sky for too many generations, the people take such things for granted, perhaps even enjoying the martyrdom, the frontier spirit, of a massive March snow. Here, at least, near the sea where the laws of physics embodied in the Atlantic moderate the climate, it only rains.

Good weather for ducks, goes the old saw. Haw, haw. But it is not apparent that the ducks like this weather any more than the birdwatchers and other hobbyists who ply the rim of the marsh in their cars, keeping dry on the asphalt margin between wetland and pine woods. Through the rain one hears the crash of the surf, improperly loud inasmuch as the Midwestern storm blows eastward. Out beyond their brown perimeters of grass, turned copper by the rain just as the

73

pale lichens on the pine boles glow green, the waters host little visible in the way of ducks and geese. A pair of shovelers dutifully shovel along in the shallows. A hundred yards farther out, widgeons widge forlornly. A few Brant geese huddle near the shore, and here and there, along the channels, crouching great blue herons glower at their formerly promising territories.

Fog arises as the rains temporarily calm down. Islands of *Phragmites* grass, scrubby myrtle shrubs, and a loblolly pine or two emerge, only to disappear in the changing mist. Sky, water, and land are one in the vapor – all is obscurity, stillness. The only mobile form of life visible is a mystery gull, undeterred from some irritable duty, whomping along into and out of view. The world might easily end in grey.

Day two.

A clear sky, whipped into purity by a wind from the northwest. Diamonds glint from the vast expanses of water. The loblolly pines and the myrtle bushes are full of little grey birds – neither a flock nor a community, but a host – flitting here and there, up, down, back and forth, chipping high-pitched chips. Is this their normal manner or is it a case of the observer observed? They are myrtle warblers, named such for their preference for the berries of the myrtle bushes so prevalent around the marsh. Every birder has seen them; they are the most numerous warbler in the east. No big deal, but it is pleasant to walk along and have them dance before me.

Out in the water, a group of ten shovelers proceeds with dignity. Who appoints the token shovelers on a day of fog and rain? Where do the malingerers hunker down for a day off? Widgeons in discreet couples, and pintails, make their genteel way through the water, as do the black ducks.

The wind gusts unpredictably across the light sky-blue shallows, darkening their surface in evanescent brush strokes. A new artist at work here today. Beyond the shallow water, the brown cord grass is bent every which way, an unkempt hairdo in need of a brush. The wind does its best to achieve order, but the scalp of this place will before long sprout new green hair, more amenable to training. Dead grass rattles quietly in the wind.

A great heron looks imperiously at its domain, then disdainfully at an approaching observer, and lifts into the wind, ritually tucking its head back on its shoulders, and leaves. Noblesse oblige.

Most of the swans and geese have left for the north. Except for a few teal, most of the spring migrants are still well to the south. There are a few exceptions to the casual, even bored, activities of the regulars. Two otters do a snake dance in the water, like Nessie, and discreetly vanish behind a hummock of grass to dally unflagrantly. Red-breasted mergansers predict the maypole, leaping a few feet through the air to dive in unison, the dolphins of duckdom. The wind makes my eyes water.

Probably no one truly understands such a place. Certainly I don't. Except for wind and, more distantly today than yesterday, the sound of the surf, it seems a quiet place where nothing much is happening. Limbo. It awaits the migrants. Now we are between times.

Once there was no such thing as this marsh as I see it now with its variety of vegetation, its wondrous tweedlike texture of brown-through-tan grasses. That is because just a few million years ago there were no grasses. They hadn't evolved yet. God knows what marshlands looked like then. And now the marsh is being invaded, pushed out.

Today is a cool but sunny, gusty spring day. Tomorrow the forecast calls for the high sixties, a foretaste of summer. That's March for you. It can bring you winter one day, spring the next, then summer – in any order.

I wander the perimeters of the salt marsh not understanding much of what is certainly going on here and am reminded of the daddy of us all: Time. It shows up as moments – as when a frog ends its brief life in the long mandibles of a heron – or as an endless spiral. Leading where? Who knows?

To begin with, the marsh asks nothing of me. It is certainly no place now to get on with a desultory birder's life-list. But I confess that I am distracted and a bit worried about myrtle warblers, disorganized but all doing the same thing, hundreds of little yellow-rumped genetic programs looking for identical niches in this ultimately temporary marsh. What will their descendants do when the myrtle bushes ebb?

And what do I look for? Today, nothing more than the marsh, as unprepossessing as it is, with nothing much happening of an epochal nature. Just the marsh and me here today, and however trivial that may seem, in terms of my particular life-lists, it is enough.

Kaleidoscopic April

I T   I S   A   T I M E of raging streams of enzymes and hormones, a universe of chemical decisions, turnstiles of free choice amid an inevitable pattern of emergence, fecundity, growth. The yellowing of goldfinches now casting off the grey of winter. A crimsoning of house finch rumps, a nattering of blackbirds choosing up sides.

The enzymatic congress of a peach tree dispenses siting laws for buds of either leaves or flowers – proletarians and sex symbols – and improbable specks of light green emerge from dry fragile twigs, an announcement of bridal gentility soon to be, followed by a reception for the bumblebees.

On its way north, a pigeon hawk (known to be a magician of sorts and lately dubbed a merlin) swoops arrogantly into the yard. A robin screams, feathers fly, and the merlin, having failed, seeks dignity in a wild cherry tree, only to be evicted by a far larger red-tailed hawk whose hegemony in this territory is simply not to be challenged. The great hawk war brings silence. Not a songbird moves until the monarch leaves the cherry tree and soars away to continue its patrol.

Water stands in a depression in the lawn. The pasture is leaning to marshdom. The sump pump gorges in the basement, filling the tunnels of moles in the lawn with unwelcome floods. Out beyond the pasture, the beavers revel in the creek's high water, unmindful of their cousins' underground nightmares. Earthworms have visions of Armageddon as the blade of a spade explodes into their lives. They curl and slowly thrash in the unaccustomed light. The world, for worms, has gone mad.

Cardinals applaud the arrival of April with insistent, piercing voice. Daffodils, the loyal workaday yeomen of spring, nod approvingly. In the gardens, now the horticultural equivalent of Cologne after the War, peonies thrust upward, angry-looking red shoots. Defiant. The exogenous cacti, flattened by frost and drained into a purple mat clinging to the rocks, begin the hydraulic task of resuscitation. Before long, erect and green, they will set forth flowers more improbable than even their ability to live in so inappropriate a place.

Water. Warmth. Day length. Fitness. Insurgency. Everyone is part of it.

Go ahead: plant your peas. There might be a recidivist frost as late as early May but the peas can take it – the Green Berets out there in advance of the army of salad vegetables, the rangers, guerrillas, pioneers staking out the scene of manifest, if temporary, destiny. April promises civilization.

Projects bud in the mind, both proletarian and sexy. Fix the rotted beams in the front porch, now sagging with besotted mischief. Attack an insidious vine that wants to strangle a young cherry tree in the hedgerow. Dig the hole for a small pool that will reflect the moon. The moon knows all there is to know of such stirrings. Pay the taxes. Take up yoga. Mothproof your tweed jackets. Transplant a bloodroot or two from the forest to a shady part of the garden. Go ahead: get in on the great, getting-up dawning.

But then there is a knock at the door.

A congenial man reports that he was sent by the local animal shelter. He found a bird, injured, on the road. It is a flicker, breathing hard, a spot of blood on its beak, head lolling in shock. How elegant, how well-dressed is this bird, a tasteful flamboyance of yellow in the wing and tail feathers, a touch of the brightest red, and shining black eyes that now asks *why*.

Long warm fingers, my wife's, envelop this mystery, a bird that seems larger close-up than one would expect from having seen it a bit more distantly, darting among the evergreen trees. It is a cosmopolite breed, wandering far to the north beyond the point where most woodpeckers dare go. Its feathers are in demand by the Hopi Indians of Arizona, for making prayer offerings that urge the invisible world of spirits to see to the health of all creatures. A bird of power, but the power resides in the bird's finale, the Hopi say. I disagree.

It opens its beak, breathing painfully, though we are told of shock syndrome and how wounded animals are unaware of pain. The gazelle, they say, feels nothing as it is overtaken and felled by the cheetah. I am not so sure, looking at the flicker's emptying black eyes. Perhaps I project on this tweedy little machine of nature my own bewilderment.

The long warm fingers remain motionless for an hour, hospice-like, hoping that the bird will at least know, shock syndrome or no, that as it dies it bespeaks elegance, a fineness beyond the murmurings of evolution. Abruptly the bird shrinks, though it still breathes. Will is gone. And quietly it dies. A cheering woodland call has been stilled. It's not the end of the world, the end of wilderness. It is natural enough, I suppose, harmonious in a way, but disorienting as well.

A bit lost, I take the bird from Susanne's hands and put it, for lack of a better place, in a Chinese dish some thousands of years old, filigreed with paint, a kind of immortality, a convenient urn of respect, a covenant perhaps.

April.

Redolent with the universal chemistry of growth, awash with promise of verdure and life, breezily and damply providing a foretaste of succulent vegetables and the harmonies of birdsong and smiling days, April is nonetheless a fragile time. A beginning . . . but also an end.

In that great getting-up morning, fare thee well, fare thee well.

Mutual Dependence

You don't have to walk very far in the country to find teeming examples of the mutual dependence of the things of nature (of which we, of course, are a sometimes recalcitrant part).

Indeed, biologists are rapidly coming to the conclusion that cooperation of various sorts – among a species or between species – is as important a flywheel in the engine of evolution as competition. No biologist observing a pack of wolves or a pride of lions on the hunt has failed to note a cooperation that bespeaks communication and maybe thought far beyond what we normally afford beasts. Sometimes what looks like a nasty bit of business (and a pack of wolves must seem nasty to an old moose) often has a pronounced component of cooperation. Out in the country one often sees a hawk being pestered unto dismay by a bunch of little birds who fly around it squawking and occasionally pecking it until it goes away with the air of an irritated aristocrat. Many owls have their daytime snooze interrupted by such annoying gnat-swarms of lesser birds.

The little birds are risking their necks to rid the neighborhood of what they perceive to be a threat, and some species of birds literally specialize in this mobbing behavior, as it is called. Among them are black-and-white members of the tyrant flycatchers, aptly named. Kingbirds have been known to harass a crow (which is much larger) to the point that they will land on the crow's back while both are in flight and peck it on the head.

Of course, one can understand why members of one species might form a posse to rid the town of a suspicious stranger. Even if one of the posse gets dinged, the rest will survive to produce more of their kind – free, temporarily at least, of such interlopers.

But consider this:

It is early July and the yard is full of fledglings and yet-to-be fledglings of all kinds. Suddenly there is a violent, raspy hue and cry from several of those felonious dandies, the blue jays, all screaming at once. A crow flies like an arrow, dark and ominous, out of the yard and into the pasture, bearing in its beak something small and evidently still alive: a baby bird. The jays pursue but stop at the edge of the yard, screaming, but suddenly a handful of kingbirds swoop past them like a squadron of fighter planes and chase the crow into the field, veering and diving at it. They are almost immediately joined by a smaller squadron of redwing blackbirds who are, like kingbirds, known to get indignant at crows.

The crow lands in the middle of the pasture and while it goes about its grisly business, the two squadrons dive overhead, finally landing to form an outraged circle around the crow, all still calling out, bobbing in anger. Before long the crow takes off with some part of its booty in its beak, pursued again by the blackbirds and the kingbirds, and flies to another pasture where it apparently has its own nest. The posse keeps up the din out in the pasture while robins hop about in the yard in their slightly imperious postures as if nothing whatsoever untoward had happened. Calm as can be.

The crow returns to his first spot in the pasture pursued by the alliance, and lands again. The others dive and swoop at him and then they too land again in a raucous and feckless circle. Suddenly a band of purple martins which live several hundred yards away begin dive-bombing the crow. Eventually, having eaten what was left of the kidnapped baby, it flies off with all three bands of birds in pursuit.

Quiet returns to the pasture and the yard, the way an uncomfortable silence can settle after the shelling of a town in warfare. It was a tragedy – a tragedy of the sort that dispassionate scientists say is simply the sort of thing that goes on in nature. Yes, indeed. Prey and predator. It has been found that wolves, for example, are not vicious killers (for all their tactical genius) but help the moose herd by weeding out the weak and the sick. And old Uncle Moose goes into shock and doesn't feel a thing and the rest of the herd races off unmindful. That could be true, I suppose.

But the case of the crow seems different. It's clear that a lot of different birds were upset at the kidnapping. One assumes that none wanted a big predatory thief about. This is not hard to understand. But the jays, relatively big birds and thieves themselves, were only angry enough to sound the alarm. The robins could not have cared less. And the kingbirds, pugnacious daredevils much like the guerrillas in Afghanistan, battled on. What was in it for the blackbirds that live way at one end of the pasture or the martins that live far off at the opposite end? In fact, purple martins are rarely seen engaging in mobbing behavior; they don't even employ much in the way of alarm calls, typically relying on nearby blackbirds to be the neighborhood watch. Why did they all ally themselves in a joint, if ultimately futile, defense? All of the birds were of one taxonomic order: the perching birds. But there were five different species involved, five different genuses in fact, and four different families – which is simply to say that a purple martin, upon reflection, probably doesn't give a damn about perpetuating the genes of a kingbird. I've never seen a purple martin pay any attention to anyone other than their own condominium-dwellers, except for a direct interloper into their private, happy ghetto. Yet there was this wonderful alliance. Maybe that sort of thing happens all the time and I simply haven't noticed it.

Nevertheless, this unfortunate drama I witnessed on a hot July afternoon – after its horror wore off for me as well as for the birds – struck me as a mysterious and exemplary bit of cooperation, a suggestion of the finest potential for us all, and I am proud of the kingbirds, the martins, and the blackbirds. And I look at the robins and say: Where were you when the chips were down?

Slackers.

Our Lads

THIS IS A STORY of a crime.

They arrived one July in a disreputable sprawl of skin and bone, clinging to a dark and sooty nest in the fireplace. *Chaetura pelagica*, chimney swifts – common enough arrivals in the affairs of human beings through some inefficiency of their species in fastening nests to the insides of chimneys. Featherless infants squalling for parental care, sounding like locusts. Four of them – one dead and the others more than likely doomed. The odds in life may be six-to-five against, but with orphaned baby birds the odds are infinitely worse.

As usual, Susanne went immediately to the rescue, plunging herself into the unknown exigencies of chimney swift motherhood. The creatures were gathered up, nasty nest and all, and put into a cardboard carton, while I headed for the bookshelf.

Insectivorous birds: Therefore the first step was to puree beef, add a touch of water and a little milk for calcium and, with an eyedropper, stick the puree into three open beaks. Chimney swifts are among the hardest bird orphans to feed because of their infernal head waggling. A miss here, a successful squirt there, and in a few minutes the screeching subsided. A chancy beginning.

Every hour they squalled and the puree was applied. Swifts fledge in thirty days. When did they hatch? Since they were featherless on arrival, we assume less than a week ago. Three weeks of dawn-to-dusk hourly feeding?

A few days passed and the birds began to show signs of feathers – follicles and fluff. The feathers came and the birds gained in size. I read up on the swifts. They are, like everything under the sun, wonderful beings, however little we know of their lives. Assuming for the moment that the babies survived, they would be capable of flight clocked at up to thirty-five miles per hour. They would spend virtually all day in flight, soaring and swooping, batlike, after insects such as beetles and flying ants and airborne spiders. In the best of circumstances, these ragamuffin infants could live for fourteen years, during which time they could fly as many as a million and a half miles.

After a week, the babies' eyes opened and they stared at their mother with a total lack of expression, yelling for food. Imagine finding that your mother is about a thousand times bigger than you. An impossible standard.

Swifts are gregarious, roosting in groups of up to ten thousand, descending an hour after sunset into huge industrial chimneys like clouds of smoke in reverse action. They inhabit much of eastern North America in spring and summer, and winter in the upper Amazon basin in Brazil and Peru. Brazil? Peru?

This feeding is hopeless, we think. One gets its bill stuck shut, being sloppy with the puree. *Sturm und Drang* as warm water is applied. Another small crisis resolved. They continued to grow, turning sooty dark; short, stubby bills frowned at us, gibbety-gibbety, demanding. They traveled with us in the car as much as a hundred miles without protest.

When it was time for them to fledge, we learned, they would be able to fly across the room. We should then put them, the experts said, on a telephone pole. They'd climb to the top and take off. But where would they go at night? By even contemplating such questions, we realized we had reached the point where maybe the odds were only six-to-five against.

After about two more days, the swifts took to popping out of the wicker basket that early on had replaced their altogether disreputable hovel of a nest. They would hop onto Susanne's shirt, glaring like three upside-down bats, then climb upward into her blonde hair. Sharp, spiny tail feather tips stuck out like a comb, the swift's equivalent of a mountaineer's crampons. Little needles that could make you wince, but just the thing for clinging to the side of a chimney or to a surrogate mother.

Would they know about catching insects? Susanne swatted flies and occasionally substituted them, or mealworms, for the beef. They liked the beef better.

On the seventeenth day, Susanne bore them outdoors clinging to her shirt. It was a windy day, with the sun peering out between mountainous clouds. The birds climbed onto her head. They looked expressionlessly at the world. Overhead chimney swifts soared and swooped, along with barn swallows and purple martins. We thought it might do these preschoolers some good to have a glimpse of their ultimate role, but seeing the athletic grace going on overhead, we believed that there was no way our orphans would be equal to it.

At which point, one of the swifts, the one that had a suggestion of eagle in its countenance (or so we thought) and that had refused a morning meal that day, took off from Susanne's head. It flew low over our yard and the next, headed for a large tree, swerved, and sailed up into the clouded sky. The wild swifts gathered around, flying with it, soaring on scimitar wings. And our swift, flapping a bit frantically, took up its life in an altogether new medium, the sky, airborne, beautifully flying, among its own. We could pick it out because it appeared slightly larger (beef-fed, after all) and because it flew with its tail spread out, the novice sacrificing speed for security.

It flew. We cheered and hugged.

The swifts and their cousins circled the neighborhood, tiny dots high in the sky. And Susanne and I watched for more than an hour, wondering why no symphonic crescendo accompanied this event, then knowing there *was* such an accompaniment – the silent burst of our own joy and awe and, yes, pride. We knew that an inconsequential birdling was now at home, that the others would follow, engaged in majestic flight, and that as soon as they got their tails together, they would become anonymous members of their race, taking swift-type risks at swiftian odds. Soon, with any luck at all, they would be in the upper Amazon basin.

Under federal law, raising foundling birds of certain species is not legal unless you have a license. We don't. But criminal as our act was, we now vicariously share the feeling of flight – a parental feeling if you will. And every summer for several years now we have been able to look into the clouds and say, "Hey, those are our birds!"

And each spring, we think again of the gift we received from those sooty little birds: a direct connection with one of those great and mysterious cycles of the planet.

Fossil Aerodynamics

THE LOCAL BLUE ANGELS – chimney swifts, of course – make their last passes of the day, perhaps their last of the season. They are scheduled to leave soon for the upper Amazon. For three of them, we think especial prayers. Tonight they all swoop in tight formation over the porch and soar vertically up and over the roof. Any minute now their place will be taken by a handful of bats, frantic ghosts in the dusk.

The changeover to the night shift forces attention on the idea of the air as a place to make a living, an ecological niche. Thinking of evolution and niches, it seems straightforward enough (particularly to someone so at home on the ground as I am) that a long time ago some fish hauled themselves out of the sea and tentatively took up life on land. This is a reasonable, plodding sort of development. But to take to the *air*... what a radical thing for an animal to do.

We've done it, of course. During a startlingly brief interval of time (even if you look as far back as Daedalus), engineers answered our urge and gave us proper engines and wings – bingo – just like that. Cultural evolution runs apace, even accelerates, but biological evolution doesn't make such quantum leaps, regardless of argumentation among theorists of this realm. A pair of lizards simply doesn't all of a sudden spawn a bird, any more than engineers were able to go directly from a Conestoga wagon to a 747. There had to be lots of incremental steps along the way and, in the relatively stately pace of bird evolution, most of the steps are lost to history. There are comparatively few fossil remains of birds and fewer yet of their reptilian ancestors, or protobirds.

The brightest jewel in the limited tiara of bird paleontology is called *Archaeopteryx*. It was a creature with a reptilian bone structure adorned with feathers in all the right places including the tail. It dates back 140 million years to the Jurassic age when dinosaurs and other charismatic reptiles including the airborne pterosaurs ruled the earth.

Pterosaurs, along with dinosaurs, crocodilians, *and* birds, all derived from ancestral reptiles called archosaurs. Pterosaurs were one strain of flying animal, birds a separate one. The air – as a niche – has beckoned often. Pterosaurs originated at about the same time as birds but took a different approach to life. They remained reptiles to the end, for example, and their reduced back legs made them almost hopelessly incompetent on land. Protobirds developed protofeathers, probably as a heat-regulating device, and most of them continued to be adept on land. (Geese, ducks, and some shore birds, by the way, are the only creatures alive that can handle all three niches – land, water, and air.)

In any event, just how some archosaur got far enough along a new path to be *Archaeopteryx* has challenged paleontologists since its remains were first found in Bavaria more than a century ago.

Archaeopteryx almost got dethroned a while back, by the way. In early 1985, the noted astronomer Sir Fred Hoyle threw the world of paleontology into shock. The fossils that show *Archaeopteryx,* the first true bird known in evolutionary history – perhaps the most significant fossils in the world – were, he said, frauds, a hoax.

Tipped off by an Israeli electronics expert, Hoyle and some colleagues had examined specially made photographs of the fossils and claimed to have found a spot or two of glue, among other irregularities. They charged that the fossils' discoverer, Karl Haberstein, flummoxed the world of science in the 1860s by adding cement to the fossils of some dinosaur-like reptiles and pressing chicken feathers into the cement, making the feather impressions. The Piltdown unpleasantness echoed ominously. The Chickendown hoax?

"Codswallop," replied a spokesman for the Museum of Natural History in London.

Nonetheless, paleontologists double-checked. Among other reassuring details, they found that, under ultraviolet light, fine hairline crack and inorganic bits of manganese run across both the feathers and the tail, proving a common – and ancient – origin for both. No glue. Hoyle remains suspicious.

Said the museum's spokesman: "I don't know why people who are eminent in astronomy or physics think they can write papers about vertebrate paleontology. Perhaps it's because we all get dinosaurs in our cornflakes." So astronomers are invited out of paleontology, but aerodynamicists are welcome. Lately some of these engineering types with spare time on their hands have stirred up the archaeopteryxian pot quite nicely. Both groups are satisfied that *Archaeopteryx* could fly, however clumsily. Indeed, the very existence of feathers defines it as a bird.

But sometime earlier, some reptile had to have become preadapted to flight, and this does not mean that some preordained evolutionary plan had already determined that certain creatures were to start the process of becoming fliers. Each adaptation that an animal makes must usually confer a *current* advantage in a *current* environment. A bird with half a wing can't fly.

The most popular view among scientists has been that protobirds began as tree-climbing animals that developed the capacity to glide on forelegs that had become primitive airfoils. Like flying squirrels, they would glide down to a tree to forage, climb it, and glide down to another – extending their foraging range with a minimum use of energy. Rudimentary flapping, increasing the foraging area yet further, would soon lead to horizontal flight.

On the other hand, it also seems possible that a protobird might have become a bipedal runner (as did many reptiles) and also gradually developed winglike forelegs that served to give the animal a bit of lift, more speed with less energy, and maneuverability as it chased insect prey. Eventually, as its pectorals strengthened, it would take to flapping its wings as it ran – like a goose – and over the generations one day find itself flying. This possibility is advocated by a team at Northern Arizona University.

Furthermore, the Arizonans say, an airborne glider would run into aerodynamic problems if it started flapping its wings. Specifically, a wing designed for flapping gets its thrust from the outer third and thus tends to be longer and thinner than a glider's wing. Technically speaking (which sometime cannot be avoided), a powered wing needs a high aspect ratio and the Arizonans can't see the incremental steps of evolutionary change bridging this gap. In other words, an arboreal glider that began flapping its wings would be wasting a lot of energy – like a parrot with clipped wings – and before long would be weeded out by the ineffable business of natural selection.

Not necessarily so, says Ulla Norberg, a Swedish scientist. She and her team (ornithology seems to have grown up: it's done by teams nowadays) have subjected the mathematical equivalent of *Archaeopteryx* to rigorous aerodynamic modeling via computer and found out how fast that once and future bird had to flap its wings to extend its gliding range to a helpful degree. About six flaps per second would do it – but that, Norberg then found, was what a same-sized bird does today and presumably no neophyte flapper could have achieved that rate.

Still, there is an intermediate kind of flight between gliding and flapping and Norberg believes that she has shown its feasibility. If *Archaeopteryx* flapped its wings down fast and then brought them up slowly, it would get all the thrust and lift needed with two wingbeats per second. Flap-gliding, the Norberg team says, is akin to a long glide down and then a quick climb, a highly efficient way to use energy employed by many birds today while foraging from tree to tree. The undulating flight of a goldfinch is much the same thing, and up to twenty percent cheaper in fuel cost than horizontal flight.

But, the Arizonans counter, modern birds don't actually use the Norberg fast-down/slow-up wingbeat, not even those which undulate in flight. If it is so efficient, why isn't it used now? Furthermore, the Arizonan calculations for the lift and thrust of such a wingbeat come out differently than Norberg's. So the question remains up in the air – where it belongs.

I'm delighted that the aerodynamicists are getting into this act. Mathematical models are terrific and they may get us closer to an answer. Math always adds zest to a game, if also a certain elitist incomprehensibility. And the nice thing about this kind of paleontological game is that it's never over. We'll never know for certain how reptiles came to be birds: it will remain a natural wonder.

Meanwhile, the bats are still flying noiselessly overhead in the night and some pest of an insect has bitten me several times. I wonder how *they* got into the flying business.

Tropical Fancy

It must be about 4:00 a.m., and I wake yet again in discomfort. I'm not used to sleeping in a hammock, and this one, I am embarrassed to report, was ineptly slung and has sunk to the point where the army of scorpions I know to have gathered on the ground below can, if I move ever so slightly, attack the tender regions of my backside. I freeze, even in half-sleep.

It isn't simple discomfort that jogs me toward wakefulness. It is the sound of a faraway locomotive. But this is the Amazonian rain forest: no locomotives in these parts. What I'm hearing is the fabled sound of howler monkeys somewhere in the distance. This is close to where the chimney swifts we raised go for the winter. But I haven't seen any of them.

Monkeys howling; dawn still far off; more hours to spend in this sagging hammock. Somewhere nearby, separated from me by mosquito netting and humid air permeated with lethal insects, my wife is evidently, outrageously, sleeping through this trial.

Beyond her, somewhere in the dark, are scientists. Biologists. Tropical biologists, who sleep through the howlers and who love every aspect of this place, even the tarantula that turned up at dinner last night, an unwitting guest of folk who seek to preserve a bit or two of this ecosystem in spite of the rapacious gleam in the eye of their fellow man. The tarantula knows nothing of man and nothing of ideas like ecosystems. It just turned up, to be enthusiastically inspected, identified, and then ignored like any properly registered specimen. I have thought about that tarantula a few times, here in this hammock. In some other group it could very easily have gone unseen or been hysterically executed, but this is a camp filled with people who insist upon loving all of God's creatures – the true pro-lifers in our society.

Still groggy in spite of the howler calls, I try to reconstruct the evening's conversation. Much of it dwelt upon the destruction of life by the razing of the rain forest. Exactly how fast these lands are being deforested is not known, for this is very remote country. Nevertheless, some people have estimated that if the current rate of deforestation keeps up, we'll be virtually out of tropical rain forest by the year 2000.

Earlier we had picked our way among charred logs, now turning to dust, where life once teemed. We trudged along behind field biologists who, on behalf of the Brazilian government and the World Wildlife Fund, are compiling a census of the life forms in isolated segments of rain forest, the better to understand how these life forms really work together and how much rain forest must be left intact for the cycle of cooperation to continue. We are about fifty miles north of Manaus, the slightly disheveled capital of the Brazilian state of Amazonas.

For now, the biologists sleep. They are soldiers in a quiet war, paid slave wages compared to placekickers in the NFL or owners of hamburger franchises. (Hamburger gluttony is one of the reasons for the current onslaught on the world's rain forests: kill the forest, clear-cut the trees and burn them, grass emerges which feed cattle for some five years before the soil gives out, then move on.) Consider the McStinct burger. Without rain forest, *my* swifts will perish.

I look for ways to distract myself, to slip away, at least mentally, from my ominous surroundings. Since what lies beyond my mosquito net is sheer, raw, unforgiving life, I can be forgiven some predawn fantasies. I half-dream, half-remember the conversation around a gas lamp here at what might be thought of as land's end.

Among the visitors in camp is a grand thinker in biology. We'll call him I. O. Spaulding (I have changed the names to protect the guilty). Spaulding is a specialist in ant and human affairs, as conversant about Madonna and human myth as about social insects.

SPAULDING: If we could get hold of the defense budgets for the world's nations for one year, we could pay off the entire debt of the Third World, pour one million dollars into saving each of the one million species that are most threatened with extinction, and still have enough left over to pay a fair price per acre to buy all of French Guyana and turn it into a nature preserve.

(The tarantula, yet unnoticed, crawls up the post that supports the plastic roof over the dining area.)

STEVE FELLER *(a specialist in Panamanian trees, among other things):* One MX missile would pay the entire lifetime costs of this project out here. Think of it. Twenty years of conservation research.

AL REARGUARD *(an ornithologist wearing Rambo-style camouflage and looking dangerously large):* Hell, for what it takes to keep one wimpy molecular biologist fooling around in a lab, you could put twenty, thirty real biologists out in the field.

FELLER: We need to make our kind of biology sexy.

SPAULDING: You know who played the only macho biologist in the movies? *(All hunch forward, listening intently.)* Michael Caine, that's who. In a film about killer bees. He takes over from a general, gets a swarm of killer bees to fly out to sea, and orders the military to blow up the swarm. We need that kind of sex appeal or the tropics are lost. We need to come across as caring John Waynes.

(An ant crosses Spaulding's plate, and all pause to admire it while Spaulding identifies it in Latin and explains its taxonomic position in the scheme of ants. Spaulding is one of perhaps three people alive who could have done that with this species.)

FELLER: Hey, we're the ones who know about the tropics. Why

don't we take some kind of action? We could write all the governments of the world and say: Listen, if you don't help us save these ecosystems, we're going to put some new virus we've found into, say, the coffee supply of the world. We'd have them on their knees.

REARGUARD *(unsheathing a machete and unbuttoning a few buttons on his shirt in brash defiance of the tropical disease vectors):* I like it. The T-Team. T for tropics. Let's go for it.

Well, of course it was only a chimera, a momentary bit of madness reconstructed no doubt inaccurately amid the roar of those damn monkeys in the teeming Amazon night, a dream, a wild hair of thought between sleeping and waking. Still, I cling to the wish, however poignant, that in that remote camp on that humid night filled with the sounds of exotic frogs, the last squawks of macaws arrowing to bed, and the plaints of the howlers, there was born a true and perfect tropical monkey wrench gang dedicated to saving us from ourselves.

Imagine the possibilities. What if the tropical biologists could get their hands on the fleet of armored trucks that transport the salaries of baseball players? What if every congressman and member of parliament thought that their collective deliberative bodies would be afflicted with some pestiferous and unsightly dermatological nightmare if they failed to divert a few million dollars from building ornate monuments to themselves and to direct these funds instead into tropical biology and conservation?

The idea was so comforting that I fell asleep again in the hammock, without even a thought for the scorpions.

Fragments

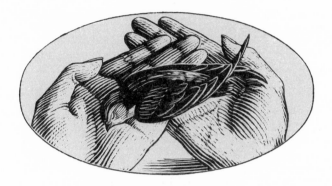

ONCE AGAIN, the long warm fingers cupped a bird, another baby chimney swift, a foster child that had tumbled down the chimney onto the hearth, pink and naked, along with its two siblings and their dark basketry, squalling and needy. We had raised chimney swifts like these in another year and felt initially confident. Insect-eaters, they would thrive on pureed beef, fed on the hour during daylight. We knew that in about two weeks they would be old enough to fly and with luck would join their kind in the sky overhead and develop the physical capacity to follow their elders to Peru for the winter.

But two had died while we weren't looking – unaccountable and dispiriting. The third looked vigorous enough, squawking for food, accepting it, growing dark feathers in its follicles; with slightly grumpy-looking eyelids, and even a certain calm as the days went by.

Then one day it wouldn't eat. It only breathed, a rapid dark bellows in my wife's hand.

Odds against baby birds are always great and we had thought of some special odds against this little protomigrant. This was taking place in August, later than a baby swift should have fledged. It might not learn to fly strongly enough before its fellows left for South America.

"I don't see how it could get to Peru anyway," I offered, but my wife's eyes were elsewhere, worrying only about the matter at hand which, of course, was life. Why, I thought, just a little angry, did they fall into our lives again, thrusting themselves on us? Why didn't the parents build a better nest, one that wouldn't fall, take care of the swiftian affairs more responsibly? What was this late clutch of eggs about anyway?

It had been some time, I reminded myself, since we had had the chimney swept. The soot had probably built up, a parlous substrate for swifts, beyond the adhesive power of swift saliva. My fault?

Swifts should know a good place from a bad one, I thought.

I should have had the chimney swept, I thought.

So what did they do before chimneys? Chimneys are only a few human generations old here – maybe ten, fifteen generations of people who have built chimney in these parts. Nevertheless, I was stuck with the fact that, however it had occurred, I had no excuse: we were the stewards in this case.

My knees were aching from squatting in front of my wife and this little bird, gamely gasping in her fingers. Abruptly, the bird shrank. It kept on breathing at the same rate, but all of a sudden it was visibly smaller.

"It's gone," my wife said as the little bird breathed on in her hand. Eventually, it stopped breathing and we buried it, feeling that somehow we had let it down. It had kept on breathing long after the moment when it evidently lost the will to live, as if the will to live was a physical thing, something with volume, the loss of which was measurable.

I remembered that years ago some Swedish physicians took to weighing people who were dying and then weighed them again immediately after death, in order to see if sophisticated measurements might reveal a minuscule weight loss, indicating the disappearance of what might be called the soul. They claimed to have detected a tiny difference but their results were not, apparently, reproducible.

I saw this shrinking phenomenon another time. It was when a man I never knew well enough was in a hospital and became stricken, entering a coma. He was suddenly smaller than before, like the swift, though he too breathed on, and I knew he was gone before the helpful and generous people in charge produced electronic evidence that his mind was gone. Sustained technologically, he breathed on, but I had already marked his passing and said good-bye as best I could at the moment, feeling among other things another failure of stewardship.

I was a little bit angry too. Why now? What is this? The schedule is not right. He was my father and, in the last few years, we were getting to know each other again after a long period when our lives were separate, estranged. Before long, after he diminished physically and was in a coma, the family and the doctors and nurses conferred and we all decided to continue to provide oxygen to him, but not to actively pump it into his lungs. This is a fine distinction – fine, I think, in both senses of the word. He was on his own.

Something – some internal spasmodic grit – kept him gasping unwittingly for almost another twelve hours, long after what I take to be his will to live, or perhaps his immeasurable spirit, had left him. Only when he quietly stopped breathing was he pronounced dead, but he had long been gone.

I had a brief look at his yellowing shell, but of course it is not for a corpse that one grieves. It is for an incomplete history – in this case the rebirth of a friendship that began too late for the entire migration to take place. But then migrations are circular and are always cut off at some point along the way. A small bird had taught me something about such passages and in a way had prepared me for this other one.

How strange it is, this life and its ambiguities, its paradox of confidence and woe.

Spider Coming Down

Canyon Diablo is a dry gash in the Painted Desert, a little way north of Route 40, that runs like an arrow between Winslow, Arizona, and Flagstaff. It is high country, a mile above sea level, and some twenty-five thousand years ago it was the recipient of debris from a meteorite impact that created a major tourist attraction, Meteor Crater, a dramatic hole and the scene of the finale of a pleasant science fiction movie, *Star Man.* I have a small dense hunk of that meteorite, and like to think of it as a piece of falling star. Everything in this region has a kind of time-warp about it.

More recent events have enclosed Canyon Diablo within the borders of the Navajo Reservation, but every spring a Hopi priest, whose reservation is inside the Navajos', goes out with youths of his clan to patrol Canyon Diablo for the nests of golden eagles. The priest knows generally where to look, for eagles are as traditionally minded as are the Hopi: white droppings on the side of the canyon are usually a giveaway. If the priest finds an active nest, he repairs to a small shrine (a place I wouldn't notice without his pointing it out) and leaves a small gift, like a piece of turquoise, along with a prayer that all goes well for the mother eagle and her offspring.

In June, the priest returns and a youth is lowered over the edge of the canyon (which is some three hundred feet deep) on a rope. The young man swings down about fifteen feet and perches on a ledge, reaches into the nest, and takes out a young eagle – a cottonhead, they call it, among other names of greater respect, since at that time in its life it has white down covering its crown. Leaving another gift of thanks to the mother eagle – who all the while may be wheeling up and down the canyon emitting high-pitched cries – the priest takes the eaglet home to the mesas where the Hopi villages sit above the desert, lonely places of a special vibrancy for a thousand years.

At dawn on a morning soon thereafter, the priest's clan members gather and the women give the eaglet a name, in the same manner that they name human children. The eaglet's cottony head is ritually washed; the young bird is presented with a perfect ear of corn to serve as its mother; it is presented to the rising sun, father of all creatures; and then it is installed on the roof of the priest's house in the village, near the plaza, and given traditional gifts that Hopi give to all their children. From the roof, it will watch the day-to-day activities of the Hopi villagers and observe them as they do their ceremonies in the plaza. Later it will be sacrificed, "sent home," to carry messages to the spirits that the Hopi have done well (if indeed they have) and deserve rain.

For a time there, in the village, the bird is not only a member of the family, but a kind of demigod – a messenger to the gods. It is faithfully fed rabbits or other animals, specially caught in its behalf so that it need never corrupt itself by having to kill. After it is sent home, its wing and tail feathers become part of the religious paraphernalia that will persist in the village for generations. Its down feathers are tied to special sticks and become prayer offerings that will carry Hopi prayers for health and the long-lasting fertility of the land, to be placed in homes and pickup trucks and innumerable shrines around the Hopi land.

For the Hopi, the eagle is part of an all-encompassing and eternal gyre of life, an inseparable feature of a spiritual and natural tapestry that includes all and sustains all. There is an entire clan called the Eagle

Clan who are charged with protecting the spiritual and territorial perimeters of the Hopi – a big job. It is impossible to isolate such a creature – or concept – as an eagle from so interwoven a web of belief and behavior and to study it, much less eliminate it, for everything is of a piece. Even so, the use of eagles is an aspect of Hopi life that is discomfiting for someone brought up on the ideas of conservation. Susanne and I went along with Hopi eagle gatherers several times, collecting eaglets, and we simply had to put our own views out of mind as best we could. We were reassured by the fact that the Hopi had been doing this for about one millennium, over and over, in the same canyons, high on the same cliffs, and the eagles persisted. The existence of Route 40 and Meteor Crater tourism a few miles south of Diablo Canyon probably exerted a more dangerous force on eagles than a succession of Hopi priests. Still, it was hard to take.

Susanne came to know one such eagle especially well. It was eventually given the name Hyouma, or Spider Coming Down. It was caught before it had had any experience. It was deified, raised above the rest of its contemporaries, and put on a pedestal of sedimentary rocks in a village called Shongopavi, where it played its role with an ancient dignity, displaying a face of harrowing perfection while all through the early summer it observed Hopi ceremonies – which have been called the most awesome works of art on this continent.

Behold: Old ladies in shawls sit quietly on folding chairs. Kids in T-shirts do their heedless thing, darting here and there in the dust, then pausing, their unexplainable motion much like that of fish in a tank. A mangy dog of many hues and untraceable lineage slinks across the open space, unnoticed and unloved. This plaza of sorts is bordered on four sides by seedy one-story houses of stone or cinder block. All around are the unmistakable signs of we usually call poverty. (But nothing is really as it seems. Anything can be transformed, as the alchemists once assumed, the magicians know, and the physicists have proved. There is no true poverty here.)

This Hopi village is perched some six hundred feet up on a yellow mesa above a desert floor which itself is more than a mile above sea level: the high country of northeastern Arizona. Within minutes the plaza has filled with spirits, maybe forty of them, bedecked in buckskin moccasins, pine boughs, white cotton kilts; bronze bodies all streaked with the same earthy colors; with multicolored, beaked faces, eyes glittering from slits. They chant like a low, distant wind while a drum thumps, metronomically adjusting the people's pulses. Turtle shells go *plok-plok* and sleigh bells go *chink-ch-chink,* fixed to the monotonously stomping legs of the spirits as they dance this way, turn, dance that way – over and over, rattles in hand.

All day in the sun, punctuated by short breaks, the spirits dance their slow, outlandish dance. Even without understanding the words or the symbolism, an outsider can get in the swing of this hypnotic spectacle. The kids, however much they dart about, are awed by these spirits, called *kachinas*. The older spectators know things are not as they seem: the masked dancers are their own flesh-and-blood kin. One day, when they are about eleven, the kids will learn that too. They will learn at their time of initiation that, with the proper preparation, these uncles and fathers of theirs can don the masks and embody the spirits, *become* the spirits. And as the dance wears on through the day, the clouds will rise up above the sacred peaks one hundred miles to the west and break off, hastening toward the Hopi mesas and the corn fields in answer to the kachinas. And more than likely it will rain.

The wind gusts up in the plaza, little clouds of dust swirl and fall, and it is clear why so many people have always believed that the wind is alive.

Taking note of all these elements, and no doubt impressed by the antiquity of the place, art historian Vincent Scully of Yale pronounced these kachina dances the most profound art form in North America. If this is so, it is because this is religious art, sacred art. In almost all its aspects, a kachina dance is a gift to the spirits and, at the same time, a formal demand that the spirits return the favor.

The kachinas like to come to the plaza and dance, embodied in the men of the village; they are asked to call forth some rain and other blessings in return. There's no sense lecturing Hopis about meteorology. Their get-togethers with the spirits have worked for centuries, and the outsider, overwhelmed by the sounds and the colors and the monotony of the ceremony, may even get a glimpse, the slightest taste, of this other kind of reality.

At which point, all hell breaks loose. A band of the most appalling ragamuffins descends in rowdy disarray from the roof of a building. For the rest of the day, these ill-clad and loud intruders will try to disrupt the ceremony, buffoonery and slapstick gradually becoming outright grossness – ribaldry gone wild. The crowd loves it. Laughter ripples out in competition with the solemn chant of the kachinas.

An outsider is thrown completely off balance, the glimpse of spirituality shattered like a mirror.

The rowdies are called clowns. They are fierce as well as funny, going about their mischief with a scary irresponsibility. They like to haul white visitors into the middle of the plaza for some not-so-gentle humiliation. It took me a long time – many kachina dances – before I began to perceive some sort of pattern in all this. Later, a Hopi friend explained that the clowns are the equivalent of our Everyman. (The Hopi word for clown, *tcuku,* has a second meaning: "to make a point.") They do virtually everything backwards, or wrong, and they become progressively more degraded, acting out the increasing corruption of mankind. They gossip, they fight, they covet things, they commit adultery, they are gluttonous, they succumb to the most serious hubris of taunting, even emulating, the spirits. In the end, under threat of death, they repent.

It's the same every time, all the antics being variations on a single theme. And it *is* funny. Coarse but funny. The old Hopi ladies hug themselves with barely controlled mirth as each earthy sin unfolds.

We don't seem to do much of that sort of thing in our ceremonies. For all our talk of blood and passion, our liturgies are a bit "above the waist." I've never run across any yuks in the hymnals and prayer books

I was brought up with, and the Bible is one of the most rigorously humorless books I've read. Whenever our animal nature becomes an issue in our religious observances, it is deftly skirted. In church, standing before our God, we tend to be an earnest lot, reverent, awed, buoyed, perhaps joyous – but only half there.

Things may have been a bit looser in medieval times when human nature, with all its biological essence, was rather more difficult to look past. In those little town/cities, everyone probably knew everyone else, knew who was making passes at someone's wife, and probably made fun of the transgressors right there in church – just as they do at a Hopi ceremony, which is a bit medieval itself and likely one of the last places on earth where a fart and a belly laugh are acceptable parts of the liturgy. The Hopi clowns are themselves kachinas, which is to say that during the ceremony they, too, are invested with spirit – divinely inspired.

Laughter is a gift, joy another form of prayer. For the Hopi a smile is sacred.

The complexities of Hopi culture have fascinated Western man ever since the Spaniards ran across what they fervently, if briefly, believed were the seven cities of gold in the 1540s. A current bibliography of scholarly works about the Hopi contains about as many entries as there are Hopis on the tribal rolls. In probing the tip of this ice flow of data, I've found nothing about the Hopi sense of humor – and no explanation of the relevance of the clowns to the kachina dances. Perhaps, to anthropologists, the clowns have seemed to be an aberration in an otherwise orderly conceptual tapestry, a world view of awesome coherence and symbolic richness.

Another reason may be that humor defies analysis. It is like the little patterns you can see if you close your eyes; you can only see them peripherally, and if you look at them directly they drift away. Similarly, any effort to define humor results in humorlessness.

Yet another reason why most scholars ignore the earthy humor of the Hopis may be the fact that science, too, is humorless. If there's anything less funny than the literature of religion, it's the literature of science.

It must be hard to be a Hopi these days. The pantheistic nature of their view of the world hardly meshes with the conceptual juggernaut of science. Hopis have to be bicultural. I once stood with a Hopi man in his village, looking out across the desert to the San Francisco Peaks rising to the west near Flagstaff. Clouds were streaming from the mountaintops, and my friend volunteered that he understood the meteorological explanation for the phenomenon and that was well and good; but, he went on, "we also believe that clouds arise over the peaks when the kachinas are there rehearsing how to bring rain." The acceptance of such opposites comes easily to many Hopis I've met, and it may be in their nature.

Linguists have opined that Hopis speak the language of quantum physics. At least in their ceremonial language, past and present seem the same tense and the future is now, in the sense that it already exists in the urgings of the heart. Given these odd tenses and the peculiar Hopi way of talking about spatial matters, some linguists say Hopis have a mental "grammar" that would make the Max Borns and Werner Heisenbergs of the world feel right at home. For Hopis, things can be in two places at once, and something can be (not *mean*, but *be*) two or more things at once, just as photons can be either matter or energy depending on what aspect of photons the quantum mechanic is inquiring about.

A lot of physicists, especially older ones, tend to get a bit poetic, even mystical, sensing the hidden unities that underlie the kaleidoscopic events of the universe, but you'll find very few of them who will postulate God. Physicists would really like to be able to explain things without resorting to such a being, and cosmologists have explained to their temporary satisfaction not only how the universe arose, but how it arose out of nothing and by plausible physical laws. Yet there seems to be some sort of preexisting mathematical design (urge?) underlying this orderly creation of everything from nothing, and one can imagine that some day soon physics and theology might become the same course. We might even become pantheists again and ask eagles to be not just objects of our stewardship but demigods.

Meanwhile, back at the quantum level of the very small, it seems that something like an electron can exist at one location in one instant and at another location in what amounts to the same instant, having changed location without really moving, having arrived without "cause." Things *can* be in two places virtually at once. Subatomic particles – at least some of them – can become altogether different things, depending on how we look at them.

To see something that way, to turn a situation into something it isn't merely by changing one's viewpoint – this kind of surprise sounds just like the essential ingredient of humor. In this sense, the insight of the quantum physicist is indistinguishable in kind from the insight of the humorist. Is the creation a joke, then?

Some physicists, having observed the mutually "knowledgeable" behavior of separate particles (they seem to keep track of each other's spin), have suggested that the universe may be one great big thought. And some physicists have suggested, a bit anthropomorphically, that humans (and in particular, one assumes, physicists) have evolved the kind of brainpower they enjoy in order that the universe can reflect upon itself consciously.

So suppose the insights from quantum physics are an accurate reflection of the reality of things – with all the sense of surprise, of things not being what they were just a moment ago. Then perhaps it is not unseemly to speculate that the universe is one great big and partly *mirthful* thought.

Maybe the Hopis are right, in their observances of the Creator, to take note of our whole nature, including that uniquely human quality, humor. For that too is part of the message the eagle takes to the spirits.

The Voices of Nature

Silver whistle at vespers from a distant woodland – a sweet, melancholy sound. It brings to mind the pipes of Pan, otherwise called the *syrinx* after the nymph who evaded Pan's ardor by becoming a stand of reeds.

The liquid trill from the woodland is not from panpipes but from a hermit thrush, one of the preeminently beautiful bird songs in the world. In fact, it is two songs, each harmonic arising from a different side of the bird's voice box. There is no way a human being with something so ill-equipped as a larynx could duplicate this sound. It takes a particularly well-developed syrinx, which is the name anatomists, with a rare sense of poetry, gave to this avian organ.

The song of the hermit thrush is, of course, not intended for our ears, no matter how beautiful we find it. Nor are all the chitters, cheeps, hoots, shrieks, howls, grunts, growls, roars, bleats, barks, snarls, purrings, croaks, whistles, and hisses that are just some of the voices of nature. These are the sounds of animal communication, an urgent business with no small talk, upon which we can eavesdrop and wonder, parsing them for meaning and content, as humans must always have done. But it wasn't until the last few years that we had much of an idea what this cacophony of nature was all about.

Alas for the gentle naturalist, it took technology – machinery – to find out what all these voices were expressing. High-fidelity equipment, supersensitive microphones, tweeters and woofers of the highest quality, but more important, a machine called a spectrograph that makes a two-dimensional drawing of sounds on paper – a voiceprint – breaking them down into their component frequencies, so that by seeing them we could begin to hear properly.

Only then did we notice the subtle phrasing of the humpback whales and realize that these massive beasts use a kind of rhyming system as a mnemonic device to recall the syllables and phrases of these haunting advertisements of self. With such hearing aids, we found too that elephants let each other know their intentions by means of moaning calls like simple songs below the threshold of our own hearing; that certain monkeys seem to use what almost amount to words; and that, with our naked ears, we had never heard the true musicality of bird song. We never knew that birds – even little ones like wrens – bark.

Yes, bark. Like dogs. And for the same reasons.

In fact, it seems that all mammals and birds, pets included, share a common "grammar" of expression. Knowing it allows us to peer through the opaque membrane that has always separated us from the rest of the animals and find out what is on their minds.

You can call it the Growl and Whine School of Communication and it's basically simple. Just about everyone has seen one dog threaten another. It raises its hackles (looking bigger), pulls its lips back (so as not to injure its lips if it bites), and it growls. The growl is a low, atonal sound – a scratchy unharmonic mess of a sound – and on a voiceprint it shows up as a dark, vertical bar with rough edges. The more aggressive the dog gets during its growl, the more the thick dark bar slopes downward to the right, getting lower as the fractions of seconds pass.

On the other hand, the threatened dog may well be terrified. It cowers (looking smaller) and whines – a high, tonal sound that shows up on the voiceprint as a thin ascending line.

Back in the late 1970s, a young ornithologist, Eugene S. Morton, at the Smithsonian's National Zoo, began to think about this when he listened to the sounds made by some Carolina wrens he was keeping in his office. Morton was enamored with the tropics, where songbirds tend to sing year-round, as does the North American Carolina wren, providing the trapped ornithologist with a pleasant reminder of fairer climes than can be found in the intemperate zone of Washington, D.C. But he began to listen to the *chirts* his wrens emitted and noticed that they varied considerably. And that was not supposed to be.

Ornithological canon at the time held that all such bird calls (short one- or two-note sounds), as opposed to bird songs, were always pretty much the same for a given bird species. Morton believed his ears and applied a spectrograph.

He already knew from observations in nature that a wren defending his territory from another wren would emit a low harsh sound, and that a wren that was the loser in such an encounter emitted a high-pitched call as it fled. The *chirt* of a wren seemed somewhere in-between – a kind of alarm call – but voiceprints of the *chirts* showed that they differed a lot, ranging along a continuum between low and harsh to high and tonal. Located in about the middle was a *chirt* that, on paper, looked like a chevron: it went up and then suddenly down. And this was the sound a wren made when it appeared to have noticed something interesting – like a distant predator or a distant piece of food. This chevron-shaped *chirt* was a sound of attention, alertness. It said, in effect, "I see something and I'm not sure whether it is something I'm going to appease or something I'm going to threaten."

It was suddenly clear to Morton that many of the sounds animals make might fit into a common system of expression. For if, as he soon showed, you record the bark of a dog and make a voiceprint of it – the very sound a dog makes when it is alert and undecided (barking dogs do *not* bite; growling dogs may well bite) – it shows up as a chevron.

Before long, Morton was poring over a blizzard of voiceprints of a wide range of mammals and birds, as well as checking out the emerging results by the relatively simple means of walking around the zoo. And sure enough, from elephants to rabbits, from herons to songbirds, some fifty-six different mammals and birds all "growled" when hostile and "whined" when either friendly or in need of appeasing another animal. And they all had their own version of the bark.

It stands to reason, after all. Mammals and birds both evolved from reptiles which in turn evolved from amphibians, and those are the only four classes of animals that make vocal sounds. And just as the ear evolved from a primitive part of the fishes' gills, so you would expect that there was something in common between all vocalizers. But reptiles and amphibians (like frogs) all keep on growing throughout life, while birds and mammals with very few exceptions (elephants come to mind) stop growing around the time of sexual maturity.

Now the voice box of a frog, say, keeps on growing with the rest of the animal, and the physics of all this dictates that the older the frog, the lower its call in pitch. (A bass drum has to be lower than a snare drum: a matter of size.) So a bullfrog, harrumphing in the night, is making an honest advertisement of his size, and therefore his age, to females looking for a mate – or to other male frogs trying to establish a place from which to call females. The big frog with the lowest voice gets both the best place and the female, while a littler frog knows not to try muscling in lest it get in an energy-consuming (and doomed) fight.

In frogs then, the actual acoustical nature, or structure, of the call is the message. Low = big (therefore old and therefore an admirable survivor) while high = small (and therefore risky, unproven).

On the other hand, the oldest stag or tiger or wren may not necessarily be the biggest. But, in order to avoid costly struggles over territories or mates, there is an advantage in seeming bigger. Most hostile mammals and birds raise their hackles to appear larger than they are, but most mammals and many birds are either nocturnal or live in places like trees where they cannot readily be seen. So there is an obvious advantage in making a low sound – a growl – if one is feeling hostile. It says, to anyone who might be around: "I'm big and I'm mad," even if you are only mad.

So, as mammals and birds evolved, their vocalizations changed from being mere statements of size to statements of what might be called mental state, or motivation. Baby mammals and birds generally make high-pitched cries (very small voice boxes can only make high-pitched sounds) to appease their parents and "persuade" them to bring food. It is a short series of steps to an adult, wanting to appease another adult, making a higher than normal sound – like a whine.

Since the very form or structure of the sounds were an indication of mental state, Morton called all this the Motivational-Structural Rules, and other scientists soon found that they applied widely among mammals and birds. Like a good scientific hypothesis, these M-S Rules not only proved universal, but they made certain predictions which could be tested. For example, they predicted that the more complex an animal society was, the more variations there would be along the continuum of vocal sounds between hostility and fear, between growls and whines, between aggression or aversion and appeasement.

Some wild canines of South America proved to be a perfect laboratory for a test of Morton's prediction. Bushdogs are little, low-slung doglike animals that travel and hunt in packs. Maned wolves are long-legged, large-eared creatures that lead solitary lives except in mating season. In-between are crab-eating foxes (really more like jackals) which hunt in pairs or very small groups.

The infants of all three species whine, eliciting parental care, and all adults growl when in hostile situations. But adult bushdogs have an elaborate set of whine variations, each variation matching some subtlety of mood and the need to maintain contact with other members of the pack in the dense ground cover of the forest. On the other hand, maned wolves have a greater repertoire of low-pitched harsh sounds, essentially a variety of ways this solitary animal can say "keep your distance." Intermediate on the continuum of both vocal sounds *and* social complexity is the crab-eating fox.

Similarly, crabby people tend to use gruff sounds, while those ogling babies tend to speak in high-pitched tones. It is no accident at all that, universally among human languages, a question ends with the voice rising. Much of human communication harks back to events that were set in motion when the first amphibian opened its mouth and grunted into the air.

It takes a lot of practice to disguise one's state of mind, especially to people who know us. Actors, a few politicians – some people can disguise their tone of voice sufficiently to get away with a lie. Gestures, the signals of body language, are even harder to disguise. Most animal communication is unavoidably honest, including vocal communication. Deceit among non-human animals may well not exist: science moves on.

The hissing goose highlights this dreadful, inevitable honesty. A female goose whose nest full of eggs is threatened by a fox is almost surely of two minds. She is aggressive on behalf of her offspring's interests and also scared of being attacked by a dangerous predator. If she were to emit a vocal sound, a goosey growl of hostility, she might betray herself with a simultaneous squeak of fear. Then the fox would know he probably had the upper hand. So geese have come over time, in such situations, to duck the issue and hiss: a nonvocal sound that bespeaks no emotion whatsoever. The hiss has come to be associated with a posture of threat (raised wings, with which a goose can inflict a lot of damage), thus getting the ambivalent goose off the hook.

One of the difficulties scientists have long had in understanding animal vocalizations arises from the very fact that scientists, being humans as well, are so uniquely talented with human speech. A major difference between our speech and animal "talk" is that the sounds we use to make up words and the meaning of those words rarely have anything directly in common. *Papillon* and *butterfly* are utterly different sounds but mean the same thing. They are arbitrary: any sound would do if two or more people agreed on what it referred to. Because of this quite natural human bias, we tend to look for things similar to language in animal species – a Lion-English Dictionary, for example. Not until Morton's Motivational-Structural Rules came along did we realize that the content, for animals, was in the sound. Form matches function in all things biological: birds that eat seeds have thick beaks for crushing, while hummingbirds, for example, with long skinny beaks, probe flowers for nectar. It is the same with the sounds animals make. Form and function are wed.

Nevertheless, the temptation to look for something akin to human speech among animals is nearly irresistible. Chimpanzees, a gorilla, even an African grey parrot, have been taught to use what we call language: words making sentences. Only the parrot can do this vocally: the apes don't have the equipment to mimic human speech. They have instead used sign language and other nonverbal systems. As interesting as all these experiments are, however, they don't tell us anything about how animals actually communicate in nature. They are basically artifacts of *training*. In nature, do any animals come close to using words?

African monkeys called vervets have been found to use three quite different alarm calls when a band is approached by a predator. They use one call when a leopard or other four-footed predator approaches, and the alerted members of the band all take to the trees, where they are much faster than a leopard. If an eagle flies overhead, there is a different alarm call, and the band heads for the thick brush, or for lower branches of the trees. And if a vervet sees a large snake, it uses yet another call, and the band members all rise up and look at the surrounding ground. This would seem to be highly semantic, and we can take some pride that it occurs among monkeys, those (however distant) primate relatives of ourselves.

Until, that is, we find that something similar happens among some lowly rodents – ground squirrels. These highly social animals live in colonies and also have an oddly specific array of alarm calls. An approaching coyote elicits one sort of call and all the ground squirrels head for a burrows – any burrow. But a badger (which is also a good burrower) elicits a different call and the ground squirrels all head only for burrows with a back door.

There is a tendency to think that the monkeys and the squirrels have invented these calls in a somewhat human manner, just as we invent new words to match new situations – for example, *computerese*. A certain squeak means "badger" and everybody seeks out the right kind of burrow. More likely, from the standpoint of evolution, is that this particular escape pattern came into being as ground squirrels that were successful in avoiding badgers probably produced more ground squirrels than those that didn't, and the particular alarm call came to match the escape pattern – in a sense, to be part of the escape. The advantage to the caller? More of its near kin, and therefore more of its particular genetic makeup, would survive. Biologists call this altruism, but it's really just nepotism.

Form and function again.

Morton's rules, by the way, apply to relatively short-distance calls. What of long-distance communication, like bird song? What are we to make of the audacious inventiveness of a mockingbird, improvising riff after new riff in the light of the moon? (Is it fair to speculate that some insomniac musicians lolling around New Orleans on a steamy night learned about improvisation and, ultimately, jazz from this Louisiana state bird?) One ornithologist attributed an aesthetic sense to birds with large song repertoires. For such birds, repetition of the same old song would in essence be boring, while inventing new songs would have *interest*. Scientifically, that doesn't get us very far: it is even harder to prove an aesthetic sense among birds than it is among humans. It is easier to disprove, in fact, and experiments have now shown that female birds do not pay attention to the variations in a male bird's song. What attracts females in the breeding season is the amount of time a male bird sings.

Most birds – especially little ones, which most songbirds are – live on very short energy reserves. A male bird that can afford to sing at length, rather than scrabbling around looking for food, obviously has staked out a salubrious territory, one that is rich in resources that will be needed to raise the female's impending young.

Then why did the elaborate songs of some birds evolve? The Carolina wren will learn about forty different songs in its lifetime. Why bother when all that is needed to attract a mate is to burble the same note over and over? The answer appears to lie in the form – the structure – of the sound.

Armed with precision equipment, many ornithologists would try to get a perfect recording (or voiceprint) of a bird's song. They would tape it from as close as they could get; they might even create an ideal voiceprint with pen and ink, getting rid of all the fuzzy edges. But a bird does not hear the ideal song from a neighbor; it hears a degraded version, because the intervening trees, air, wind, soil, even temperature, change the sound. Again, Gene Morton flung himself into this, trying to figure out what the listening bird got out of hearing a degraded song emitted by one of his fellows nearby.

It turns out that what the listener gets is an idea of how close his neighbor is. And that's important to a bird that would be better off looking for food than racing off to the edge of his territory to repel intruders, thus using up precious energy.

It works like this. Take a wood pewee: it has basically one song. It says *pe-wee*. Now, locally, all the pewees sound almost identical. A listener knows what the ideal *pe-wee* sounds like, and some part of its brain can tell from the amount of degradation of a neighboring *pe-wee* how far away the singer is. Similarly, a Carolina wren may have some forty songs but his neighbors know most of them, and know how they degrade in the woodlands where the wrens live. They have a mechanism for assessing distance based on the difference between some template of wren songs that they have learned and what they actually hear from a neighbor. (And it has been found that only males have this capacity for assessing distance by the nature of song degradation.)

If the listener's distance assessment is wrong, he will probably misjudge the whereabouts of his neighbor and waste precious time. How would you mess up such a mechanism? One way would be to learn a new song or a new variation of a song, something slightly unfamiliar to your neighbors. Another way would be to adapt your song acoustically so it degrades as little as possible in the local neighborhood. Both would make listeners think you were closer than you actually were.

But alas for the romantics among us, imagining panpipes and avian affairs of the heart and aesthetics, that is what bird song appears to be all about. In evolutionary terms, elaborate bird song came about in an arms race between the role of the singer seeking to confuse his neighbors and the role of the listener playing catch-up and developing more accurate distance assessment.

It has been shown, for example, that a Carolina wren can be so disrupted by the sound of a song that it cannot "range," that it will cease foraging activity altogether for a protracted period of time. And in the parlous months of winter or any other time of stress, such inactivity can be fatal – also allowing the singer to aggrandize nearby territory.

It would seem, then, that the more elaborate a bird's song, the further the evolutionary arms race has proceeded. The riffs of the mockingbird are not a matter of personal aesthetics, or of dazzling a potential mate; they are a kind of warfare. And the less inventive but indescribably beautiful harmonics of the hermit thrush are sung not for thee, but as a threat.

Such findings lend a slightly lonely cast to these purposeful little lives, but it by no means needs to diminish the sense of beauty that we can serendipitously derive from them across the boundary between their universe and ours. And when we think from time to time of how we ourselves imbue our words with meaning by our very tone of voice, we can recall where *that* came from and perhaps marvel a bit at the urgency and honesty of the voices of nature – a world which, for better or worse, is free of small talk.

The Golden Travel Guide

ONE OF MY FAVORITE travel books is an old and worn-out
Golden Field Guide to the *Birds of North America*. The pages are falling out; the book is not only dog-eared but dog-gnawed (by an innocent puppy), its corners now round. It never leaves the house. In it my
wife and I have noted the first sighting made of any bird (except birds
like robins and crows that everyone has seen since childhood).

Neither of us is anything like a fanatic birder, a person who will
drop everything and drive hundreds of miles because a Ross' gull (normally seen in the Arctic) has strayed into Boston Harbor. I have no
particular desire to race around and see all eight hundred or so species
in North America; I wouldn't drive to the southern tip of Texas just to
see an Altamira oriole or, in fact, go anywhere simply to see a bird.

But almost everywhere I go, for business or pleasure, there is the
delicate tracery of color and movement birds provide. They are almost
always on the periphery, at least, of things, and usually when I go
someplace, there are new birds to be seen. And once seen, they are entered in the beat-up Golden guide, which serves as a mnemonic device
for recall of many places, many trips, over many years. Since it was my
wife who got me interested in birds in the first place, the field guide is

also a kind of record of our marriage – a different kind of journey, but a journey nonetheless.

Early on, my wife-to-be took me on dawn patrols of the Chesapeake and Ohio Canal outside Washington, D.C. On one such expedition – my first, in fact – I peered through the branches of a bush and saw what I soon learned was called a prothonotary warbler. I was hooked. I can look it up and find that it took place in the late spring of 1974 at the Pennyfield Lock of the canal, and can feel again the heady days of courtship.

The pages of the guide fall open to the rose-breasted grosbeak, and I am in the land of the Hopi in December 1974, my first trip ever to the Southwest, much less to an Indian reservation. I am sitting nervously inside a Hopi house a day after driving through a strange, lava-strewn landscape and arriving in this remote spot. It is freezing outside, bone chilling and bleak. We have just seen a sign outside one of the Hopi villages, a near ruin perched on a mesa top, that explicitly bans white people from the premises.

In a bush outside the window of this Hopi house, a black and white bird with a swatch of pinkish red on its chest appears, which we later determine has to have been a rose-breasted grosbeak, even though the field guide's map says this is mostly an eastern bird. Seeing the bird in the guide brings back the smell of piñon logs burning in the house and the feeling of strangeness, humility, almost hopelessness, as we began a project to document Hopi life, a project that would take eight years and call for nearly thirty trips to the reservation. These trips would come to define a great portion of our lives and interests, and the grosbeak is an emblem for me of those shaky, slightly nerve-wracking beginnings.

There is a category of birds called peeps. These are little sandpipers— shorebirds that go *peep* and, to an even more than casual inspection, all look alike. The requirement to distinguish among peeps is what keeps a lot of people from becoming serious birders. I no longer have the patience (or the eyesight) for it, but the painting in the guide of a least sandpiper brings back a trip down the California coast and, specifically, the town of Castroville, which claims to be the artichoke capital of the world. The main street was lined with large, green plastic artichokes. I wonder if the least sandpipers still live nearby and if the plastic artichokes are still there, or if the residents finally rose up in revolt against such silliness.

Turning a page forward in the guide, I am reminded that it was also in Castroville that I saw my first phalarope, in this case a northern phalarope, a sandpiper that spins in circles in shallow water to stir up food with its thin bill. Thus engaged, it looks no less improbable than streets lined with giant artichokes.

A few pages further on, a notation beside a white-headed and black-tailed gull (Heermann's gull) reminds me that our next stop after Castroville was at Point Lobos, south of Carmel. I recall how beautiful my wife looked to me, striding among the magnificent rocks and tidal pools. This in turn reminds me that we next drove through Big Sur, a place that the poet Robinson Jeffers and others have extolled but which gave both me and my wife an inexplicable case of the creeps. Discovering we both felt this way after the long, silent drive, we wondered if a lot of Indians had been killed along that coast.

White-tailed kite. Bam. Sacramento, back in the heady days (for an environmentalist) of Jerry Brown's governorship. We were on our way to a meeting with the governor and, turning off a freeway onto a cloverleaf, I looked up at what was obviously a white angel hovering over the greensward. I pulled off the road, much to the exasperation of the other drivers, and watched the angel. Eventually it flew off. We looked it up in the book and then went on to meet the governor. For some reason the topic of highways came up. Jerry Brown thought there were too many highways – and too many planned. When I told him, however, that cloverleafs provided good hunting grounds for white-tailed kites, he thought I was mad.

Birds of prey, such as kites, appear to have little in common taxonomically with ducks, except that they are both birds. But ducks directly precede birds of prey in the field guide, and there, thumbing backward from the kite and Jerry Brown (who will always inhabit page 67), I come upon the harlequin duck and the notation "Esquimalt Lagoon." Until I got to Esquimalt Lagoon, which is just outside Victoria, British Colombia, I figured a duck was a duck. But in the seething water between the entrance into the lagoon and the Strait of Juan de Fuca, I saw this astonishing duck that looked as if it had been painted by a master clown. Furthermore, it looked shiny, as if it had been varnished. It stayed in the entrance, bobbing violently up and down, and I nearly fell in the water, so beautiful it was.

This was my awakening to the variety of ducks, a kind of mini-epiphany on a rainy day near Victoria, which itself struck me as a place of great beauty, every house having a yard full of flowers even though it was November. I have heard since that the harlequin duck can live in calm water, but it prefers fast-running streams and turbulent surf, where it pries the likes of shellfish out from under rocks. A kind of Type A duck.

The field guide reminds me that I have seen an albatross – a Laysan albatross, which is not the largest of these soaring masters of the ocean air, but a seven-foot wingspan is nothing to sniff at. Hawaii. The first of the two outright vacations my wife and I have ever taken alone together. (The other was to Ixtapa, Mexico, an instant resort on the Pacific coast evidently designed by fellows with computers. They somehow designed out any shorebirds or gulls, so there is no record of that trip in the field guide.)

On the island of Kauai we acted a bit like real birders for ten days, splitting time between various habitats for birds. We got a little pamphlet that showed all the birds of Hawaii. We saw about a third, including an iiwi, a bright red-and-black bird with a red decurved bill. We were looking for such creatures in a high cloud forest, where weird branches emerge out of the mist, disembodied, and then disappear. We saw the iiwi perched on a branch for less than thirty seconds, and then it, too, vanished into the mist. Elsewhere we saw orchids growing in the cracks of tennis courts. And on our last day, having sought out remote beaches on the island, we discovered that the beach far down a cliff below our very condo was inhabited by diurnal human birds with no plumage whatsoever. All this floods to mind whenever I see the albatross and other birds that appear in both Hawaii and North America and are thus in my field guide.

Not all the associations are joyous. Located in between the albatross and the boobies are the petrels, and one of these is named Wilson's petrel. I first saw one of these small, pelagic birds from a deep-sea fishing boat off Atlantic Beach, North Carolina, while I was placing in the sea the ashes of a brotherlike friend. This little grey-brown bird emerged over the wake and pattered its feet on the surface of the water, looking for food. Then, like magic, it disappeared. My deceased friend's name was also Wilson.

A number of birds in my book, including the mountain chickadee, the blue grouse, and the varied thrush, bear the notation Cle Elum, a place in rural Washington. Here there were happier times visiting this same Wilson on a beautiful ranch where he had holed up with a collection of zany friends to write a book on energy conservation back when people suddenly realized it was a good idea.

The ruddy turnstone, a dapper shorebird that is black, brown, and white with orange legs and looks like a tweedy Princeton graduate, spells Oregon Inlet between the barrier islands of North Carolina. It was a time when we took our six daughters to stay in a motel near the Cape Hatteras lighthouse for two weeks. There was a storm and a flood, and rather than worry about it, we made little sailboats out of driftwood and held races in the flooded courtyard. The motel owner was so pleased with the example we set for the other (fretting) guests that he gave us a discount.

The acorn woodpecker, another dapper bird, means the alpine pass from New Mexico's Route 136 west to Crystal, a Navajo settlement where, years after seeing the woodpecker dart across the road, we have become friends with a local family. The two are associated in my mind, both being highly sociable and family oriented. The clapper rail be-speaks Chincoteague Island, off Virginia's Atlantic shore, where we used to go for New Year's Eve, rising before dawn to patrol the marshes for the odd frozen heron, and having to wait till noon before any res-taurants opened.

Keeping an eye out for new birds in a new place gives us, I like to think, a little bit of insight into the genius loci; keeping track of such sightings gives us an album, a reglimpsing of moments that, for one reason or another, have been dear. One day, perhaps, I will see a ver-milion flycatcher, not a rare bird, but one I have not seen. Somewhere in the Southwest where I am greatly drawn as if there were a magnet there with my name on it. In any event, I will note it down in the Golden travel guide when I see it and then, one day, be reminded of the slant of the sun or the purple of a cloud, or some small, unpredict-able adventure.

Glowing bolts of memory, other windows on a life that hurtles by, slowing things down a bit. It beats the hell out of coffee spoons.

The Hobbit's Air Force

COOL FOR DAWN on a June day, but moist. Haze turns the near-by hills to the west a pale turquoise and almost obscures the sweet sine curve of the foothills beyond. I note that the tree line on the hills will, before too many years and in the nature of trees, totally screen the foothills from my ken, and for a moment I am distracted by rude and inappropriate thoughts of anti-tree guerrilla strikes. Chain saws in the night. Mortars.

It takes a lot of human attention and effort to keep a landscape as beautiful as this one. It takes clearing, farming, the constant attention of ungulates like cows and horses, and the ruthless hacking down of weedy things like trees, or you lose the dynamic conjunction of field and wood, the edge that has a nearly universal attraction for many birds, for foxes, and of course for people. Perhaps, in our case, this is because the edge is where we seem to have become human long ago. In such a landscape you have, instead of the stately, uniform forest that the Indians had to deal with in their inward, slightly depressive woodland way, diversity and the gentle geometry of agrarian man and nature.

Some of this geometry is now obscured in the moisture of the early day's atmosphere, but I know it is there. If the spring is too wet and

June arrives too hot, it seems an unkind time for insects. Houseflies hibernate (or whatever they do) longer and are, happily, missing. Those larger flies that plague the pasture also haven't reported for work in their usual numbers. A horse, standing in the tall grass of the pasture, is at breakfast. It is a thing of beauty in the burgeonings of June. It is a bay. Someone around here knows its name, but I don't. I wonder why we assign names to anything, especially horses.

All horses are, of course, named Beauty.

There was a time when we used to equate beauty with truth. I don't know how much truth there is to horses – it is rumored that the horses we have nowadays are a bit – er, um – stupid, but they surely are beautiful. The twin concepts of truth and beauty are often separated, even made opposites. No doubt, as we regain in our guts the wisdom of the ancient Greeks, it will become apparent again that truth is beauty and vice-versa. As for horses, few creatures suggest to me so wonderfully graceful a combination of form and function, of appropriateness. It was surely no mistake that Jonathan Swift made horses the highest life forms in *Gulliver's Travels:* anything so well made, designed with such exquisite proportion, must embody something higher than mere evolutionary chance.

Still a bit sleep-laden, my mind wanders off and my eye is struck by an oriole. Lit by the morning sun, the oriole turns to fire. The male has been about for several days now, checking out the arena of his passion-to-come, calling with his liquid song. Ornithologists tell us that the oriole is related to blackbirds and grackles and all that rude and unseemly lot, but I will believe what I want about birds: the oriole is representative of fire, one of the four elements of the Greeks, shimmering bright.

Meanwhile the bay horse, only its haunches, shoulders, and back evident above the tall grass, is still. Its tail is free of the chore of swatting flies. It is all as still out there as a Constable painting, romantic but punctiliously accurate, rendered with the clarity of an eye uncluttered with uncalled-for-generalizations.

Later in the day, I hear reports of hot-air balloons easing northward in my direction – probably from the airfield at Warrenton, Virginia, where such people hang out along with other aviation-minded madmen. Some fourteen balloons, I hear, have been sighted south of here, so I watch for them. But the breeze dies and they don't come – a shame, since hot-air balloons, while primitive compared to airplanes, are far more beautiful: skyborne spinnakers in a soft, slow race to wherever the breeze goes, commanding the air but at its whim as well. The hobbit's air force.

The thought of hobbits leads me to other mythical creatures which we are no longer permitted to believe in. It seems, for example, that I should be allowed to watch the lavender edge of wood and pasture in the hope of seeing a flash of light from a quivering white haunch as a small horselike beast steps daintily into the grass – a glimpse of a sun-dazzled pearly white horn. It would be a unicorn, kidlike in size, antelopelike in grace, with the form of a horse but the power and fleetness of a demigod, a reminder of pure excellence and the elusiveness associated with perfection.

A solitary being, the unicorn would in older times appear only to one who had done well, a small gesture beckoning one to keep living well at least for one more day. We tend not to see unicorns in our pastures these days. Instead we look for numerical gauges of achievement. We are encouraged to compute career trajectories or the biomass supportable by a few acres of pastureland and convert the calculation into currency of one sort or another. But believing in something like a unicorn is nonetheless important, I think, as a standard on which to hang our daily behavior. What have I done today to deserve the apparition of a unicorn out in the pasture? How, in these days of measurement and econometric analysis, are we to be rewarded for excellence of behavior? Science may not be much help. From the Latin word *scientia,* it means simply knowledge, which is less than wisdom. We need cues like unicorns, or ospreys maybe.

How fitting it would be also to see a centaur or two. Vastly athletic beasts with human torsos rising from equine bodies, they were bacchanalians, followers of Dionysus, drunkards and wastrels to be sure, but I'd love to see a roistering group of them come thundering with animal force over the hillside to have a wondrous disorderly bash in the pasture, messing things up, reminding us that we do not live only by history and logic, but are animals too, open yet to the ancient delights of life without cortex.

The day passes aimlessly for me. In the pale blue, moisture-laden opaque sky of afternoon the sun emerges as a rather annoyed, over-sized, hot pink disk. A wisp of cloud brushes its circularity. All that atmosphere makes the sun reddish, according to certain principles of physics that are easily forgotten once found to be plausible. Then dull clouds scuttle across the sun and suddenly it seems more like an errant planet – Saturn, maybe, with tacky, color-enhanced rings, compliments of NASA, parked for a moment in the backyard. Garish. A bit like a balloon.

The balloonists have by now made some complex and inconvenient arrangements for their descent and return to Warrenton or Albuquerque or wherever they set out from, and the only aviators in sight are the birds, making the best of the end of the day. Grackles, starlings, and their ilk make spear flights from one tree to another and then to the hedgerow or the house – soloists. Robins ply the lawn, flashing colorful vests like nouveau-riche snobs in a resort. There is a tremendous amount of noise, all avian but for the green frog's minimalist bluegrass, as everyone again and again explains current intentions.

Overhead the true aeronauts play – darting, soaring, chittering musically, working over the aerial plankton: mostly airborne spiders which are themselves a bit like balloons, free-floating and easy prey for the chimney swifts Susanne and I raised and choose to recognize as ours. Three swifts swoop by, low overhead, chittering with what seems to be greetings and cheer. We return the compliment with approval of their expertise.

The cacophony of bird good-nights begins to soften. The sun, still pink and bloated, encounters a cloud or some other intervening object, and the pink disk takes on a narrow pout, a pinched frown, as if – ever the infant – the father of us all doesn't want to go to bed yet.

But it does. And in the glow of its passing there is suddenly something like silence. Only a final, pointless flight or two of blackbirds, a last chitter of swifts from overhead, a couple of tinny bleeps from the cardinal, and then, faintly, the breath of the distant creek's waterfall. Later we will hear the owls. The trees begin to take on even greater dignity – the gravity of the immobile in which the elm reigns supreme – as a light mist feeds the air over the pasture. Moisture seeping everywhere.

The night crew comes on duty. Bats ply the chimney swifts' former territory, gobbling up insects. But bats, I note with the snootiness born of association with swifts, seem a bit frantic in flight compared with the elegant maneuvers of *our* lads. Perhaps this is because birds started off earlier as fliers while bats, being mammals, only got there recently – like us in our balloons and airplanes and spacecraft.

The sun's fire is gone from the sky. Dark comes and the fireflies blink their cold sexual messages against the stars and the dark arms of the elm tree. I take a last look, and noting that all the locals are in place, go inside, hoping that the balloonists have made it back to wherever they came from.

Godspeed to all of those who ply the air, and to those who laugh, and dream fine dreams.

Afterword

SINCE THE TIME that these birdish affairs were addressed, my wife and I have followed our own migratory instincts, leaving the rolling hills and woodlands of Virginia's Piedmont for a dry mesa-top overlooking the distant city of Albuquerque, New Mexico, and with a view of some 180 miles north to south, which includes several mountain ranges. This is desert land up here and, upon arrival, it became clear that the kaleidoscope of bird life we had enjoyed in Virginia would be no more. It seemed that we would have to do without such blandishments in this depauperate area. Explaining this to an ornithological friend, I was told simply: "Well, there'll be plenty of herps."

Herps.

Great. Lizards and things like that. Worthy to be sure, and interesting. Moving west, I realized, was going to be a big change.

I soon discovered that the 180-mile stretch visible from my backyard is the center of the universe – in fact, several such centers. Earth navels, they are called as well, places where "the people" emerged into this world. Due east of me the Sandia Mountains rise up like a great crouching guard dog, named for the Sandia Pueblo tribe whose reservation prevents the city of Albuquerque from sprawling north. They emerged into this world somewhere in those mountains. Beyond this open space is yet more, stretching north almost to Santa Fe, all of it the lands of various Pueblo tribes, each of which has its own earth navel.

Like the crags and grottoes of ancient Greece, the Southwest is populated with shrines and with demigods, deities, and spirits working out to this day their heroic and mundane affairs among the daily lives of the people who can still see them. It is safe to say that nowhere in the United States is the Indian cultural presence more prevalent and deep-seated than here in the Southwest, that in no other place is the very concept of earth as mother so deeply, and routinely, felt. But this is not to romanticize Indians as "natural ecologists," and all that. There is plenty of despoliation on Indian lands – by Indians. While unalterably religious in their feelings for nature and the land, Indians are also pragmatic. Small groups of people eking out a living from the land have, generally, been smart enough not to foul their nests. Large aggregations of people and, in particular, any group whose survival is threatened, will often forget to think about the long term. Nevertheless, a sense of earth as a live being prevails in Indian country.

I can look north of here to the Jemez Mountains, and I am reminded that there are spirits there, too, though I cannot see them, spirits that bespeak an older way of seeing the connection of man and earth; legends and myths we might call them, lessons in a kind of etiquette. Rarely have I heard an Indian voice raised in any conversation. Indian voices are as quiet as the breeze playing among the rocks, telling old stories about the ways of things.

We have our own stories too, our own legends and myths – though these tend to be based on what we know to be the facts. What high school biology student has not heard the one about the moths and factories, a British tale? It seems that there were all these light-colored moths that liked to sit resting on the trunks of trees during part of their day. The tree trunks were about the same shade as the moths, so birds had a hard time finding them. Then factories were built and smoke billowed forth, and it blackened the tree trunks with soot, and lo, the moths turned dark to maintain their canny camouflage. Of course, this is an evolutionary tale. It is quite true, except for the imputation of purpose among moths. It works like this: Among the moth population were some dark ones, oddballs, whose strain was more subject to predation in prefactory days and therefore was less numerous overall. Then comes the darkening of the tree trunks, and the light-colored ones become more subject to predation. Their numbers declined rapidly (though not entirely), and the dark ones multiplied and gained numerical superiority. One can expect that clean air acts will reverse the process.

I stand in my backyard and look out into the night. The lights of Albuquerque gleam and twinkle like a great necklace in a black velvet dish. The necklace grows weekly, each twinkling light computable into gallons of water mined from the underground aquifer. North, the Indian lands are largely dark. I decide that if I were in charge of the moth population in the English midlands, I would monitor smaller, oddball strains with some regularity to make sure there were enough around in case something else went haywire. I am glad to be in a place where a small fraction of the population still holds the notion that the earth is, in utter reality, a mother – a being that needs to be dealt with by means of a fine sense of reciprocity, by means of rules of etiquette that are not that hard to understand.

Chances are it is too late for many of us to repopulate the world we see with spirits, with an all-explaining animism like that which prevails on Indian lands. But we can see the tree trunks changing all around us and surely will need to consult that old book of manners – to look on the likes of birds, perhaps, as I have tried to in this book, passengers on the same fast train we ride, worthy of our courtesy and our care, merely because they are with us.

On our mesa-top, we are not birdless, as feared. Upon arriving at our newly purchased house, we saw a raptorial bird circling it. It turned out to be the male of a family of burrowing owls that lives about two hundred feet away in an arroyo. Walking around the inside of this strange new house before the moving van had arrived, we discovered that a roadrunner had walked in with us. It took several minutes to get the bird out of the house and, in the process of leaving, it left behind a tail feather which is now on the wall. Recently the roadrunner has taken to showing up once or twice a day outside the door awaiting a handout – preferably ground round hamburger meat. It will stand patiently a few feet from the door until Susanne or I approach, at which time it hunkers down in what would seem to be a babyish begging posture. During the breeding season, it collects whatever little balls of hamburger we toss to it – up to three in one beakful – and carries them off, presumably to its young. On one occasion, when I was heedlessly distracted by other affairs, it came in the house and down the hall to where I was working and emitted its attention-getting call, a kind of low whoop combined with the clattering of its bill.

Hawks and ravens ply the area, and several families of scaled quail bop around the premises. In spring, we watch for a pair to bring its baker's dozen of bumblebee-sized babies for their first outing, and thereafter nervously count babies on these evening vespers. Nighthawks are somehow born of the flaming sunsets of summer (if the Indians don't have a myth about that, they should). Sandhill cranes pass overhead twice a year in sunlit ribbons and Vs, on their annual migration from Idaho to a refuge south of here and back, including in their number a frail handful of whooping cranes. I could, in fact, be one of the few people on earth whose roof has whooping crane guano on it.

It is by no means the same as bird-rich Virginia but it will do. I saw my first vermilion flycatcher out here. Susanne and I were visiting a spectacularly large ranch in the bootheel of New Mexico, the part that dips down into Mexico, on one mission or another. One of the hands, a former county deputy sheriff who was also an accomplished birder (no stereotypes in New Mexico, believe me) took us to a place right near the border – a man-made pond called a *tanque* beside which grew several cottonwoods.

"There," he said. "Male." A little packet of the brightest red in the world danced in the air, flitting from cottonwood to cottonwood. "Female. Right behind." I peered, and he said, "Plane."

Plane? I looked up, and emerging over the hill that separated the *tanque* from the Republic of Mexico was a World War II vintage four-engine plane, painted a uniform muddy dark green, hugging the ground. It dipped, evidently saw us standing there with binoculars, and veered south, rising and falling with the land, maybe two hundred feet up, until it disappeared. The identification was promptly made for this winged oddity. "Drug smugglers."

In New Mexico, the enormous sky is usually full of several different kinds of weather at one time and, often, representatives of the hobbit's air force – Albuquerque being the capital of the hot-air balloon. We woke up our first morning in this house to the sound of distant gunfire: it was predawn fireworks on the horizon, heralding the launch of more than six hundred brightly plumed balloons into the morning stillness.

The balloonists have to choose their windows between winds very carefully. This is a windy place, especially up here on our mesa where, as often as not, a stiff breeze slams into the mesa edge and creates a nearly visible updraft. And at such times a pair of sparrow hawks sometimes arrive, hovering motionless in the breeze but for an occasional fine adjustment of a flight feather or two, suspended about fifteen feet from me, as if fixed just at the lip of the mesa, masters of the air and providing the entire world with an indescribable lilt.

Their arrival also puts me in a mild grouch. Not that they aren't beautiful (to me and, presumably, in some birdy way to each other) and not that they don't fill the heart with awe, as well as unleashing the thought that it is only humans, among vertebrates, who can get away with being unathletic. I get grouchy because I am not supposed to call these birds sparrow hawks anymore. Some years ago, an organization called the American Ornithological Union (AOU) got fidgety about the name. The AOU also frets about which birds are related to others, often gazing about and lumping two birds – such as two orioles – into one species. This is based on various scientific criteria and it seems like both useful work for ornithologists and judgments that are beyond the ability of nonscientists. But what gets me is when they start tossing out the familiar names of birds, as often as not wreaking havoc in everyday life. The only Baltimore Orioles in the world nowadays, for example, play baseball.

Noting that sparrow hawks rarely eat sparrows, and are falcons, not true hawks, the AOU renamed them kestrels because the bird reminded them of a small falcon that lives in Europe, Asia, and Africa – i.e., the old world – called a kestrel by the British. Now I happen to be a bit of an Anglophile myself, but I don't see a need to be slavish about these things. I thinks it's fine if the AOU wants to lump species together and even tinker with Latinate names – in this case, *Falco sparverius,* which literally translates into "sparrow hawk." (And why didn't they fix *that?*)

But common names of birds are poetry, and the AOU should hire poets if they want to mess around with the *vox populi.* Since they didn't, I have declared my independence from the AOU and asserted a certain kind or frontier anarchy. I went back to an English poet, Gerard Manley Hopkins, that celebrator and master manipulator of Anglo-Saxon (i.e., real) English.

Now when I look out at the *sparverius* pair dancing their minuet in the wind that livens this mesa-top, I say: windhover.

Corrales, New Mexico
1993

About the Author

Jake Page is the author of numerous magazine articles and books, including *Lords of the Air: The Smithsonian Book of Birds; Pastorale: A
Natural History of Sorts;* and *Hopi,* which features his wife Susanne's
photographs. They are currently working on a companion volume,
entitled *Navajo.* The Pages live in Corrales, New Mexico.

Colophon

Songs to Birds was set in 11½ point Adobe Garamond. Garamond was originally designed for metal type by French engraver Claude Garamond in the sixteenth century and remains one of the most popular of all typefaces. The book was typeset by Peter C. S. Adams and has been bound and printed by Maple-Vail Book Manufacturing, Binghamton, New York. The paper is Glatfelter Antique Laid.